The Death of Dialogue
and Beyond

Edited and
Introduced by Sanford Seltzer
Max L. Stackhouse

FRIENDSHIP PRESS   NEW YORK

1969

Library of Congress Catalog Card Number: 72-102952

CONTRIBUTORS

Rabbi Sanford Seltzer, Director, New England Council, Union of American Hebrew Congregations, Chestnut Hill, Mass.

Dr. Max Stackhouse, Associate Professor of Christian Ethics, Andover Newton Theological Seminary, Newton, Mass.

Rabbi Balfour Brickner, Director, Commission on Interfaith Activities of the Union of American Hebrew Congregations, New York, N. Y.

Dr. Frank M. Cross, Hancock Professor of Hebrew and Oriental Languages, Harvard University, Cambridge, Mass.

Dr. W. D. Davies, Ivey Professor of Advanced Studies in New Testament and Christian Origins, Duke University, Durham, N. C.

Dr. Malcolm Diamond, Associate Professor of Religion, Princeton University, Princeton, N. J.

Dr. David Flusser, Professor of Comparative Religions, Hebrew University, Jerusalem, Israel

Dr. Rosemary Ruether, Visiting Lecturer in Theology, Howard University, Washington, D. C.

Mr. Phillip Scharper, Editor, Sheed & Ward Publishers, New York, N. Y.

Dr. Krister Stendahl, Dean, Harvard Divinity School, Cambridge, Mass.

Dr. Manfred Vogel, Professor of Religion, Northwestern University, Evanston, Illo

ACKNOWLEDGMENTS

The articles by Frank M. Cross, Phillip Scharper and Balfour Brickner were delivered at Andover Newton Theological School as papers. We gratefully acknowledge permission to reprint, from other sources, the following articles:

"Judaism and Christianity: Then and Now," by Krister Stendahl, published in the *Harvard Divinity Bulletin,* Vol. 28, No. 1. (1963).

"Torah and Dogma," by W. D. Davies and "A New Sensitivity in Judaism and the Christian Message" by David Flusser, both published in the *Harvard Theological Review,* Vol. 61 (1968).

"Theological Anti-Semitism in the New Testament," by Rosemary Ruether. Copyright 1968 Christian Century Foundation. Reprinted by permission from the February 14, 1968 issue of *The Christian Century.*

"The Problem of Dialogue Between Judaism and Christianity," by Manfred Vogel, published in the *Journal of Ecumenical Studies,* Vol. 11, No. 4 (1967).

"Christian Silence in Israel," by Malcolm Diamond, published in *Judaism,* Fall 1967.

CONTENTS

INTRODUCTION

More than two years after the Arab-Israeli conflict of June 1967, peace has not come to the Middle East. Armies are still poised along borders. Arab guerrilla attacks grow bolder and Israel retaliates with increasing severity. Innocent people continue to die as both sides stock their arsenals with ever more sophisticated weaponry. The geopolitical impact of the war remains clouded. And clear judgments of justice remain impossible.

Equally uncertain and, in the view of certain segments of the Jewish community, ominous is the future of Jewish-Christian relationships. Dialogue was an early casualty of the crisis. Most of the American Jewish community, both lay and religious, wondered openly whether the Christian goodwill and understanding they had come to expect was genuine or *ersatz*, a flimsy shelter of pretense torn asunder when the chips were down and the Jew turned to his Christian neighbor for support. To be sure, some church bodies as well as individual clergymen spoke out forthrightly, but for the most part churches were either silent or content with the issuance of what in Jewish eyes were bland, emasculated pronouncements.

In some instances Jewish organizations and institutions literally put their Christian counterparts on the carpet and, taking advantage of long-time associations and mutual interests, extracted I.O.U.'s from embarrassed colleagues. In other instances, Jewish organizations and institutions found themselves on the defensive as Christians demanded to know how it could be that Jews who had been victims of and who had fought against ethnically based politics, religious establishment by government, and total military mobilization of populations could now celebrate these in Israel? As a result, there were those convinced that, with the possible exception of the "professionals" whose job it was to keep the dialogue going, serious conversations had ended. Some Jews concluded that the relative silence of the churches was symptomatic of the failure of what had passed for dialogue to cope with the religious significance of Israel and the meaning of Jewish peoplehood. And some Christians concluded that they were not going to be used or blackmailed into unqualified endorsement of Israeli policy in a way that would betray what they thought was common loyalty to a trans-cultural and trans-ethnic biblical God. Clearly, not less but more discussion was necessary.

That was more than two years ago. With some exceptions, the dialogue has yet to be renewed on the scale characteristic of pre-June 1967. Old wounds have not completely healed. Old friendships remain slightly strained. Each new incident along Israel's borders reawakens painful questions and repressed resentments. More and more large segments of the Jewish community become con-

vinced that they must go it alone and large segments of the Christian community become convinced that for Israel actually to have statehood
requires a reassessment of the foundations of
political community on the part of the Jews.

I

For those of us who view dialogue as an essential component of the contemporary religious
scene, the continuing crisis merely reinforces its
urgency. This time, however, reentry into the dialogue will require a new look at a number of presuppositions. First, there continues to exist group
egocentrism on both sides. Within the Christian
community, latent anti-Semitism may be impossible to eradicate. Can Jews expect Christians to
deny the binding nature of New Testament theology, which has overt anti-Jewish moments? While
it is true that many churches and church schools
have made a serious and conscientious attempt to
interpret and even to censor some of the more
blatant passages, many Jews feel that the reread-
ing of these passages in the scriptural lesson of the
week and their reenactment in the ritual cycle of
Christian belief provides a constant if subliminal
reminder of the age-old image of the Jew as the
residue of a defunct religion, who, in rejecting the
Christ, remains a wandering representative of
hard-souled legalism. And many Christians feel
that the Jews accent notions of chosen peoplehood
or holy peoplehood in a manner which denies any
authenticity in the religions of the *goyim*. Official
Jewish bodies and scholars may not treat the
matter in this fashion, and it may be more a func-

tion of a minority trying to maintain integrity, but Christians feel it persists not only in the forms of more traditional worship but also in the subconscious psychology of even secularized Jewish communities.

Second, it was highly unrealistic of Jews, even before the war, to believe that somehow 2000 years of hostility would suddenly disappear with the issuance of the Vatican Schema and proclamations by other church bodies condemning anti-Semitism and calling for new understanding and harmony. Such wishful thinking was the handmaiden of the ensuing disillusion. Nor was the Jewish community, which expected so much of Christians, honest with itself or with its own motivations in engaging in dialogue. Frequently defensive and certainly filled with latent anti-Christian feeling, it could only react with self-righteous indignation once the short-lived honeymoon was over.

Jews do have the legitimate right to expect that before Christians deal with the question of Jew, Arab and Palestine, they make a serious effort to comprehend the dynamics of Jewish theology and Jewish history that is understood by Jews to culminate in a Jewish state after 2000 years. While in the hands of some, this implies that anything less than total commitment to Israel's cause is blatant anti-Semitism, for most it means Christians must try to understand that Zionism is more than a political manifestation, the outgrowth of nineteenth century European nationalism, however significant the latter may or may not be. The longing for Zion is basic to the historic Jewish experience.

Yet many Jews, profoundly sensitive to the legitimate grievances of the Arabs—refugees, territorial displacement, etc.—are well aware of the excesses that can be perpetrated in the name of God. It is one thing to offer prayers of thanksgiving for Israel's deliverance from Arab threats of genocide. It is another to glorify Israel's victory as an act of divine providence, to speak of captured Arab territory as "liberated" and in some circles to call for the permanent retention of these lands as part of the new greater Israel. The blessing of cannon is no less repugnant when performed by rabbis than when practiced by clerics of other faiths.

In the light of what appears to be an increasing and recurrent theme in some current Jewish publications, it needs to be emphasized that there was neither mystery nor miracle connected with the capacity of the Israeli army to defeat a force numerically greater and logistically superior. Training, tactics, dedication, a sense of virtual isolation from the outside world, the overwhelming memory of Dachau and Auschwitz, and the willingness to die if necessary are more compelling explanations.

II

The questions are both theological and political. The creation of the modern State of Israel shattered the theology of exile that had been dominant for so long. The traditional words of the Seder, "Next year in Jerusalem," need no longer await some eschatological fulfillment, but only the bureaucratic processes of obtaining a passport and

visa. What the impact of this will be upon the
Jew's conception of his identity, as well as the
Christian's view of the Jew, remains to be seen.
No longer alienated, no longer supernatural, no
longer a product of a tradition which aside from
its biblical antecedents is largely a tradition of
societal marginality conceived in an historically
hostile non-Jewish environment and yet not fully
conditioned to the reality of an Israel, the Jew
must reassess who he is and whether he can or
even chooses to be a "light unto the Gentiles" any
longer.

Christians, too, are reassessing. Clearly, the
genocidal rhetoric of the Arabs was terrifying to
Christian as well as Jew, even to those many
Christians who found their loyalties shaped by
long and deep contact with the large nonfanatic
communities of Christian Arabs. But few politically sensitive Christians thought that the Arabs
had the will or the capacity to carry out their
threats even where they would seem to have a
case against Israeli policy or history. In overwhelming numbers, Christians supported Israel's
right to exist and its right of access to the sea on
the east. But many Christians felt that they could
not allow themselves to be pressured into an unqualified endorsement of Israel's actions of the
past or present on either political or theological
grounds.

Politically, many Christians felt deep responsibility to both Christian and Muslim Arab refugees,
as did some Jews. Perhaps more important, Christians felt that the Middle East situation could not
be allowed to totally polarize the world. If Arab
versus Jew became also East versus West, under-

developed versus developed, feudal-agrarian versus urban-technological cultures, Allah versus Yahweh, Jihad versus Holy War, the stakes were too high in a nuclear age. While to the Jew this appeared as another evidence of Christian willingness to sacrifice the Jews to international power politics, to the Christians it meant that a people who have established a nation in the community of nations must begin to transcend apocalyptic perspectives, difficult as it may be, in view of the recent apocalyptic experience at the hands of "Christian" nations. Thus, Christians frequently assumed a "semidetached" view of the situation, using the same kinds of categories of analysis that would pertain to conflict between, for example, India and Pakistan.

Such an interpretation is not, however, merely political for the Christian. It is rooted in theological assumptions which the Christian now sees must be brought to the surface. Although the Jew sees the space and politics of Israel as a religious matter (held as such by practicing and secularized Jew alike), the Christian sees it as a necessary safety valve and partial, although still woefully inadequate, restitution for the Nazi holocaust. Also unfortunate is the fact that the creation of the State of Israel was brought about by a United Nations action in which the Great Powers sanctioned a kind of "eminent domain." Like much eminent domain, it occurred at the expense of a relatively powerless group. In addition to that problem of basic justice, Christians find attempts to sanctify geopolitical events contrary to their best understanding of the biblical God. Even if there are "Catholic countries," "Protestant coun-

tries," etc., there has been the continual claim in
Christianity, particularly accented in Protestantism, that no place can contain God. Indeed, in
most forms of radical Christianity, there is the
insistence that no place is more holy than any other
place. Theologically, if not always in practical
piety, no altar, no shrine, no building, no city, no
government is any more holy than any other
geographical spot. Hence the separation of church
and state, the dropping of the doctrine of sanc-
tuary except as a moral platform for conscience,
the calling of the church a "meetinghouse" in some
traditions, and the hesitation about sending dip-
lomatic representatives to the Vatican among
Protestants. And contemporary Catholic thinkers
seem to be moving slowly and painfully in similar
directions on theological and pragmatic grounds
in spite of the heavy burden of piety to the contrary.

Christian sensitivity on the theological issues,
however, has been unsettled by the Jewish indict-
ment of Christian perspectives on the Near East.
Just as Christians criticized Jews for chauvinistic
spatialized religion, Christians are criticized for
spiritualized religion that does not know what to
say when hard questions of geopolitics are raised.

III

The roots of a possible new conversation between Christians and Jews may grow out of an
attempt to get beyond the mutual indictments of
spatialization or spiritualization. And when Christians try to get beyond their hesitations about the
fertility of dialogue, they find two theological
assumptions with which they have to deal.

First, Christianity does not tend to view Judaism as a contemporary, living tradition trying to find breathing space. While it has opposed the localization of religion in space, Judaism is, more frequently than not, localized in time by Christians. There *was* a Jewish period and now there *is* a Christian period. Seldom is the matter stated so explicitly, but such sensitivities function on the level of hidden presuppositions in many Christian contexts. Colleagues in the rabbinate down the street are often still viewed by parish clergy as the Pharisees and Sadducees with whom Jesus was in controversy about the breaking in of a new age. Relatively little serious theological focus has been placed on the Christian notion of the "second coming," which would seem to suggest that Jews and Christians alike must await the messianic age on the basis of the already given promises of God. Even less serious attention has focused on the notion that God's covenant with Israel is an eternal covenant toward that new age, and that Jesus Christ is the way by which that covenant is potentially universalized and extended to the Gentiles. Both the concepts of the second coming and of the covenant have functioned in popular politics under a vulgarized dispensational theology. Yet, there are indications that such themes need not be so crudely dealt with. They can be developed to become live theological options to allow a new sense of "complementarity," and to mitigate the theologically and sociologically pathological effects of rigid periodization and exclusiveness. At the same time, these themes prevent a specific geopolitical arrangement from being seen as evidence of the Messianic age.

Second, Christianity has tended to draw a rather

rigid distinction between Law and Gospel or between Torah and Dogma. Yet the confrontation
between Jews and Christians over the Middle
East crisis is occurring at a time when post-ortho-
dox scholarship seems to be less hampered by
confessional requirements on the part of both
Christians and Jews. Common problems of historical and contemporary reconstruction made the
traditional sharp distinctions blur. The law is not
mere exteriority nor the gospel pure inwardness.
It may well be that the law must be seen as having
and as having had an inward and positive function, and the gospel must be seen as having and
as having had an exterior form and an implied
specification of moral and social requirements.

In short, the debates about spatialization or
spiritualization, periodization or common expectation and law and gospel have opened up a real, if
still tenuous, possibility of beginning serious conversation at a new level. And there are some
modest hints that the new encounter may require
both traditions not only to engage in conversation
but to reassess and even modify fundamental
presuppositions exposed within those conversations.

IV

In the fall of 1967, an ad hoc committee of
Protestant, Catholic and Jewish representatives
met in Boston to ponder these issues and to see
if it were still possible to speak to each other. Out
of these deliberations there emerged plans for a
colloquium, held that December at the Andover
Newton Theological School. Entitled "Israel, Jews

CHRISTIAN SILENCE ON ISRAEL: AN END TO DIALOGUE?

Malcolm L. Diamond

Many issues are swirling in the wake of the Israel-Arab war. The new shape of the Middle East as regards both territory and population is yet to be determined, and it is still hard to predict the long-term effect of the war on American-Soviet relations. A side issue that has emerged in the United States concerns the relations between Jews and Christians. Israel's victory has elicited admiration among many Christians who have had their stereotypes of Jewish brains jolted by this manifestation of Jewish brawn. In a fashionable apartment house in New York a doorman assured a Jewish tenant that, "We always knew ya had a bit of the Irish in ya!"; and gags along the lines of "See the Pyramids, visit Israel," receive a hearty reception in quarters that had hitherto been hospitable to anti-Semitic jokes about pawnbrokers.

In sharp contrast to this new looseness among laymen, considerable tension is being felt in clerical circles. During the continuing crisis in the Middle East the official organizations of Christendom have remained neutral. Furthermore, there have been very few expressions of support for Israeli stands on specific issues from unofficial groups of Christian clergy. A number of rabbis who have been prominent in interfaith movements have charged the churches with the betrayal of silence. These rabbis are deeply disillusioned. For years they have heard "isolationist" Jewish leaders warn them that efforts at Jewish-Christian dialogue are futile and misguided. In support of their antipathy to dialogue these Jews have insisted that hostility to Judaism and the Jews is an ineradicable element of the Christian ethos; they point to the animus toward the Jews that mars important sections of the New Testament and to the incredible persecutions of the Jews in Christian Europe. Furthermore, the machinations and equivocations of the church fathers at Vatican II show how difficult it is for official bodies of the church to expunge the traces of anti-Jewishness from Christianity, even after the Nazi era showed where this pathology can lead. There is little enough in the record for rabbis who participate in Jewish-Christian dialogues to use in answering these arguments. To counter their terrible emotional force these rabbis rely on their own experiences: the experience of intellectual illumination from such men as Reinhold Niebuhr and Paul Tillich and the warmth of personal encounters with many Christian thinkers. When contrasted with the immediacies of this kind of experience the attitude of the isolationist rabbis seems as abstract and irrelevant as the warnings of Jewish parents to a child who is dating a Christian. The parents may insist that "They're all that way," but the child encounters affection.

At the moment, many Jewish participants in interfaith dialogues are disillusioned on both theoretical and practical counts. On the theoretical level they have heard Christian thinkers express a veneration bordering on awe for Israel. Now they discover that their Christian partners in dialogue see no relation between "Israel" as a theological symbol and the "Israel" that appears on contemporary maps of the Middle East. On the practical level these rabbinic participants in dialogue have experienced arm-in-arm camaraderie with Christian clergy in both the civil-rights and peace movements. When the Middle East heated up they expected that expressions of support for the specific policies of the State of Israel would emanate from Christian organizations. When these were not forthcoming, some rabbis apparently solicited them from their partners in dialogue and encountered a changed atmosphere. Most Christian leaders were reluctant to take a stand and defensive about being put on the spot.

The anguish of the Jewish participants in dialogue is understandable, because these recent events have triggered the trauma of another Christian silence, the silence of the Nazi era. The prospects for future interfaith discussions now seem dim. They will certainly not be fruitful unless some of the deceptions surrounding the term "dialogue" are dispelled. Jewish and Christian participants have both exploited the word; they have misapplied it to superficial efforts in the field of public relations, and they have failed to realize that, even when it is properly applied to serious discussions, the word points to an ideal of communication and not to the sort of thing that can be programmed. The charges of bad faith that have arisen during the crisis in the Middle East

are symptomatic of the deeper problems associated with efforts at Jewish-Christian dialogue,
and, after a look at some of the issues involved
in this crisis, I should like to explore those problems.

Realism toward future efforts at Jewish-Christian discussions requires the awareness on both
sides that the specter of anti-Semitism stains all
contact between Jews and Christians. But realism
does not require Jews to take the line that "Scratch
a Christian, and you find an anti-Semite." Although the response of many Christian clergy to
the current crisis may be symptomatic of this disease, the charge should not be directed at those
Christians who have sought Jewish participation
in serious religious discussion. There are many
reasons why sensitive Christians who are not infected with anti-Semitism have not expressed unqualified support for Israeli positions.[1]

Turning first to theoretical considerations, we
should realize that serious theological confrontations between Jews and Christians (I do not propose to consider efforts at public relations) are an
affair of the heart as well as of the mind. The
participants share common types of educational
experiences, such as seminary training, common
intellectual disciplines of Bible studies, history and
theology; and they often share a dedication to
common standards of religious authenticity. As a
result, they develop an *esprit de corps* which often
makes them more at home with one another than
with lay members of their own religious communities. Yet these theological associations are
products of maturity. They are genuine, but they
are also less deep than associations that enable

men to communicate wordlessly out of common upbringing and out of inheriting the historical experience of communities that span many generations. In times of crisis—and the Israel-Arab war was certainly one of these—the centripetal pull of the home-communities tends to outdraw the centrifugal attractions that have been manifested in dialogue. More specifically, a crisis of this kind drives home the differences that exist between the Jewish and Christian understanding of the term "Israel."

Christianity is a faith to which individuals adhere. The various communities of Christendom are organized around their selections from the spectrum of Christian beliefs concerning Jesus of Nazareth, the Bible, and the church. These Christian communities are not organic; they do not affect the at-homeness of national and racial groupings. For Christians the term "Israel" resonates with an ideality that is considerably removed from the particularities of history. They tend to think of it in terms of "the Israel of the Spirit," a concept that is used to measure the shortcomings of all earthly associations.

By contrast, Judaism is not a faith, but a faith-people. Israel was called as a people and promised a land. For contemporary Jews this is not an allegory which deals with the spiritual quest for an ultimate haven; it is the story of "our Fathers." Each year Jews, of whatever stripe, celebrating the Seder, are adjured by the rabbis to celebrate it as though they themselves went forth from Egypt, because "it was not only our fathers whom the Lord redeemed; He redeemed us, too." The connection is integral, and it is organic. It is a

connection of consanguinity as well as of faith, a
connection to a land as well as to a Scripture.
Rabbi Balfour Brickner, one of the first Jewish
spokesmen to deplore Christian silence, expressed
his dismay at the manifest failure of Jewish thinkers to communicate this point to their Christian
partners in dialogue. This failure is not surprising.
Communication is easiest where the parties have
a great deal in common, for example, with regard
to the prophetic call for social justice. Understanding is difficult on those points at which the traditions most sharply diverge. It is about as hard for
Christian theologians to understand the Jewish
position on the *religious* significance of the State
of Israel as it is for Jewish thinkers to understand
the inner logic of Trinitarian dialectics. Therefore,
if the Christian response to the State of Israel is
restricted to the moral and political levels, Christians ought not to be charged with bad faith. Indeed, it should be noted that within the Jewish
community there are representatives of the right
wing of orthodoxy and the left wing of secularism
who urge the dissociation of this state from religion. Furthermore, Jewish spokesmen are sometimes guilty of double-think on this issue. When
rallying support for Israel they invoke religious
associations. However, if a Jew expresses distress
at Israel's divergence from prophetic ideals, they
scornfully dismiss him as an idealist who is in-
capable of coping with political reality.

On the practical level, rabbis who have participated in the Jewish-Christian dialogue are out-
raged by what they regard as one-way communication. Christian leaders seeking Jewish signatures
for petitions of protest on race relations and Viet-

nam found the lines open. During the present conflict, all too many Christian clergymen seem to have been "out" when rabbis called upon them for support of Israel. The gravity of the situation may be appreciated when a scholar like Jacob Neusner, who has been distinguished for his breadth of spirit, can write: "Some [Christian leaders] have held that Israel-Arab relationships constitute a political issue. Our support has been solicited, however, by these same people in other issues, such as Vietnam, race relations, and the like, which are no less political."[2] His conclusion? "The middle ground of religious and theological conversation has, I think, been closed by the massive indifference and, I think, craven silence of those from whom some of us had hoped for better things." Apart from the outrageous suggestion that the support of any American on a question of conscience is *solicited* as one might solicit the support of De Gaulle for our policies in Southeast Asia, this sort of moralizing raises many problems. In shifting from the religious to the moral and political levels, I do not propose to examine the merits of the complicated skein of issues relating to the Middle East. I propose to show that Christian silence, in some cases, may not be craven, but troubled, and that it is not so much the product of indifference as of conflicting moral concerns.

The searing story of the Jews in Christian Europe culminated with the Nazi episode. Many Christian leaders have been sensitive to the enormities of this history and to the culpability of Christendom. If they had not been, Israel would not exist today: the nations of Christendom played a crucial role in the councils of the United Nations

when the State of Israel was established. However, Christian guilt toward the Jews has left
Christians vulnerable to the Arab charge that
Christian Europe dumped its Jewish problem in
their laps. Many factors contribute to the intensi-
fication of Christian anxiety on this point. The
presence of thousands of Arab refugees confronts
the Christian conscience with a considerable burden of suffering, even though the Arab nations
may exploit this issue in a heartless way. Israel's
policies since the war have engendered the fear
that Arab spokesmen may be justified in charging
that the State of Israel is not only an alien force
to the Middle East, but that it is expansionist as
well. This last point is especially relevant to the
misgivings of Christians who have participated in
the peace movement. Many of them are moved by
the righteousness of Israel's position vis-à-vis
Nasser and other Arab extremists. Yet, in the re-
sort to war as an instrument of national policy
they see a menace not merely to human well-
being, but to human survival. How then can they
support Israel's demands for the retention of territory—Jerusalem or any other—as a prize of war?

Some Christians are troubled by the domination
of our mass media by the Israeli point of view. As
events unfolded in 1967 Nasser was clearly the
aggressor. He violated the understanding on the
basis of which the Israelis withdrew from the
Sinai peninsula in 1956. The American press was
saturated with the sense of outrage that we all felt.
However, there was very little, if any, discussion
of how the Israelis had happened to get into the
position of withdrawing in 1956. I, for one, am
convinced that the terrorist tactics of countries

that have refused to recognize Israel's right to exist forced its hand in 1956 as it did ten years later. Nevertheless, the 1956 collusion with the colonial powers, England and France, raised serious questions of Israel's intentions, questions which have never been very much discussed in this country. In the war of 1967 Israel played the part of David, and the Arabs were Goliath; when it comes to the matter of communications in the United States, many American Christians, who tend to sympathize with the underdog, may be confused as to which side really is the underdog in the world of power politics.

The difference between the Jewish and the Christian response to this set of considerations reflects a basic difference in historical experience. Jews, especially those of us who lived through the Nazi era, could not help feeling the clutch of terror at Nasser's talk of a "final solution" to the tensions of the Middle East. Christians, lacking the anxiety inculcated by the Jewish experience and knowing that Israel had already scored two victories over Arab armies, did not feel that Israel was faced with extermination. They were inclined to sit back and await developments. Had things gone badly for Israel, strong and unequivocal Christian support would have been forthcoming. This is part of the anguish. It would doubtless have been too late. Jewish sensitivity to the historical paradigm of abandonment in a hostile world accounts for the sense of urgency in American Jews. This explains the unforgettable unity and magnitude of the response of this American group that prides itself on its diversity and even on its factionalism.

Overriding all other considerations making for silence on the part of sensitive Christians is the fact that the timing could not have been worse. From the moment Nasser blockaded the Gulf of Aqaba the crisis was at fever pitch. Jewish leaders naturally expected their Christian partners in dialogue to urge our government to break that blockade; in concert with other powers if possible, but if not, on our own. Yet the very Christian leaders who are most active in dialogue with Jews are the ones who have been most active in protesting our government's policies in Vietnam. These policies have been protested on the grounds that we ignore the United Nations, that we act without the support of our most important allies, and that we place excessive reliance on force. Christian leaders were caught in the same bind—a sudden shift from dove to hawk—that troubled secularist liberals, such as John Galbraith and Arthur Schlesinger. Although this switch came easily enough to some doves, who gave good reasons for it, other doves demurred. My point is that men of good will differed about this issue, so that there is no need to impute sinister motives to Christian leaders who marched with rabbis in protesting our policies on Vietnam but who could not go along with the rabbis on Israel. The point may be more readily appreciated if I draw a parallel to the relations between Negro leaders in the struggle for racial justice and their white counterparts.

All morally sensitive white men in this country are aware of their guilt in relation to the Negroes, but there is no simple formula for transforming this guilt into positive support for specific approaches to racial justice, much less to support for specific tactics. A white man may be fully persuaded of his personal involvement in our national guilt, and he may nevertheless regard the black nationalism of the present leaders of SNCC and CORE as tragically misguided. On the other hand he may go along with the general approach of the black nationalists and demur on specific tactics. Yet, as soon as a white leader in the civil rights struggle dissents, on any level, some Negroes will brand him a pseudo-liberal whose prejudices are coming to the surface. I do not mean to suggest that the points at issue are the same as those between Jews and Christians, but rather that members of any beleaguered minority constantly probe their allies. Every difference becomes a test of commitment rather than a question of judgment. At moments of crisis this renders communication impossible. In light of the tragic history of the Jews in Christian Europe, Jews have the right to demand unqualified repentance of Christians as a precondition of Jewish participation in interfaith discussions; however, no one has the right to pre-empt another man's conscience.

The crisis of the Israeli-Arab war has exacerbated the problems that were implicit in the efforts at Jewish-Christian dialogue. Before interfaith discussion are resumed, it would be useful to look at the background of these efforts and to get clear as to what may reasonably be expected of serious discussions between Jews and Christians, especially on the theological level.

Dialogue has been an "in" word for almost two decades. It is rooted in the "I-Thou" philosophy of Martin Buber, which is often called "the philosophy of dialogue." We can best appreciate his ob-

ject in introducing the term by seeing what it
was directed against. Buber strenuously opposed
the use of language for the manipulation of people.
The propagandist or pitchman is the enemy of
dialogue. He knows exactly where he wants his
listener to come out. His mind is closed to the
possibility that his preordained goal of communication may be erroneous or misguided. He is not
concerned with the question of truth; he is only
interested in scoring. The people he addresses are
not partners in an open-ended exchange of views,
because he does not recognize them as persons
who are capable of influencing him just as much
as he might influence them. The propagandist regards his audience in objective terms; he works
on them just as impersonally as he operates on his
loudspeaker or on other technical facilities.

Once we are clear as to what Buber was rejecting, the positive sense of "dialogue" is easy enough
to grasp. The man who enters a dialogue is aware
of his fallibility and eschews fanaticism. He knows
that the other person carries weight. This means
that he realizes that the feedback from their in-
terchange may alter some of his own deeply
cherished convictions. When a dialogue comes off,
each partner becomes so sensitive to the other person's point of view that, in Buber's terms, he lives
through their meeting from the other person's side,
as well as from his own. It is an intensified form
of empathy. This sort of meeting cannot be programmed; spontaneity is integral to authentic
dialogue.

Another point is that issues worthy of the name
dialogue are momentous. One need not attempt
a dialogue to decide which supermarket to patron-

ize or where to go on vacation. Dialogues are attempted where the participants speak out of fundamentally different orientations, such as those of Protestant and Catholic, or Christian and Jew.

"Dialogue," then, is a highly charged word. It points to the possibility of reconciliation and extraordinary understanding between persons, but it presupposes fundamental differences of outlook and deep conflicts of interest. "Dialogue" is also a word that is peculiarly vulnerable to exploitation. Buber directed it against gimmickery in human communication, but as soon as it became fashionable it was deployed as a gimmick.

The exploitation of the word dialogue in interfaith communication involves, among other things, subsuming many kinds of communication under this one word. Publicists for our American religions have not hesitated to invoke the term when they operate at the Chamber of Commerce level of extolling "the American Way." Others have used the word for any sort of scholarly gatherings at which Jews and Christians read papers on such matters as the dating of archeological finds.

The vulnerability of the term "dialogue" to exploitation is obvious, but even when used authentically it is bound to elicit false hopes that result in disillusionment. The problem with the term is that (like the I-Thou relation of which it is a special case) Buber used it to embrace two radically different elements of experience, those that are subject to conscious decision and those that are spontaneous. I can control (within limits) getting myself in front of Rembrandt's "Aristotle" at the Metropolitan Museum of Art, but I cannot control the impact that painting has on me; there can be

no guarantee that I will have an I-Thou encounter.
So, too, Buber's use of "dialogue" in talking of
Jewish-Christian confrontations is a compound of
things that I can consciously control and things
that either happen spontaneously or not at all.
Thus I can (again within limits) consciously control my appearance at a Jewish-Christian discussion, and I can control my participation. For example, when the going gets rough I can sit it out
and try to achieve a greater degree of understanding with Christians who may be saying things that
hurt. However, I cannot consciously will my understanding of a Christian position on a point of
divergence such as the Incarnation, nor can I
consciously control a Christian's understanding of
Torah or Israel. I was nine years old when Hitler
came to power. We lived in Brooklyn, and my
parents discussed the Nazis in anguished tones
from that time until the end of the war. As far as
I was concerned, Germany was just over the
bridge, nearer than Manhattan. How do you communicate the impact of this experience to someone
with a completely different background? How do
you translate the concrete character of this experience into someone else's moral abstractions
regarding international relations? Or, to look at it
from the other side, how does someone who is
convinced that he has the right moral answer to
the Israel-Arab conflict (an answer that is not
favorable to Israeli positions) persuade me that I
am being morally blinded by the intensity of these
experiences?

Understanding is hard enough to achieve in
dialogue. Yet understanding of a "dialogic" kind
does occur. What is even rarer is a basic shift in

the orientation of the person who understands. The sort of shift I have in mind is the shift that might be involved for a Jew in changing his understanding of the Halachah and his patterns of observance, or the change in orientation that a Christian might make in shifting sides on the Trinitarian issue. If changes of this kind are rare within Judaism and within Christianity, it is obvious that they will be even rarer when confrontations between Jews and Christians take place. Dialogues will very rarely result in changes in the assessment of the significance of the figure of Jesus of Nazareth on the part of Jewish and Christian participants.

There is nothing wrong with the rarity of "dialogic" understanding or of the basic shifts in orientation that may result from it. Given the fact that these kinds of understanding and response are not subject to conscious control, this is to be expected. But there is something disastrous about supposing that, if one makes the effort to do those things which can be controlled, such as attending conferences and listening to what the other people have to say, "dialogic" understanding *must* ensue. There is no guarantee whatever that it will. Furthermore, rather than face the disappointment of dialogues that have not worked out, participants often make matters worse by pretending that genuine understanding has taken place. Divergence and hostility are then intensified as all parties don hypocritical masks.

"Dialogue" is a problematic term. With all the sincerity in the world, efforts at it can misfire. If rabbis who have participated in dialogues were more keenly aware of this, they might not have felt so betrayed. If modest efforts at intellectual communication are attempted, and the word "dialogue" is jettisoned, then the extraordinary understanding characteristic of what Buber meant by "dialogue" may emerge as a by-product, but the achievements of this kind of understanding cannot be made a part of the agenda. Furthermore, reflection on the historical factors involved in efforts at Jewish-Christian dialogue makes it clear that only limited achievements may be anticipated from future efforts at serious discussion.

If we think about both the origin and the meaning of the term "dialogue," it is obvious that one of the major efforts at it would be religious interchanges between Jews and Christians. Martin Buber was a Jewish religious thinker who talked to Christian theologians and had a great deal of influence upon them. Indeed, some of his encounters with Christians served as formative influences on his vision of dialogue as the ideal of communication. Furthermore, the intellectual and moral aspirations of Judaism and Christianity make them hospitable to this ideal. Whatever their practices may have been through the centuries, they affirm the sanctity of both truth and individual conscience. They share the view that the only commitment worth having is that of the free and knowledgeable individual.

Yet it would be fatuous to assume that a fundamental alteration in the intellectual interchanges between Jews and Christians would ensue solely because they share an ideal of communication. If ideals dominated the communication between Jews and Christians, the record should have been better down through the centuries. We should not have had the forced disputations of the Middle Ages in which Jewish leaders were dragooned into debate on a "heads you lose, tails we win" basis: if the Jewish spokesman came out second best, there seemed to be no reason why Jews should not convert to Christianity, and if the Jewish spokesman won, he subjected himself and his people to even more blatant forms of persecution. Obviously, there have been historical changes that have contributed to a fundamental shift in the Christian approach to Judaism and to the recent concern for dialogue. The basic pattern is a familiar one: a common enemy makes strange bedfellows. In this case the common enemy is secularism. The secularism that has served to bring Christian and Jewish spokesmen closer together has two prongs, the political and the cultural. On the political level the nations have insisted on freedom from ecclesiastical control. This has been a major factor in ensuring the rights of Judaism and of individual Jews. The equality that resulted is a precondition of the mutual respect that is required for efforts at dialogue. On the cultural level, both Christianity and Judaism have had to cope with the challenge of science.

Secularism has provided the preconditions of the Jewish and Christian communication that has gone by the name of dialogue. But the impetus to it came from a different quarter. The events of the Nazi era confronted the Christian community with the enormity of Christian guilt toward the Jews. Today, many Christian leaders are concerned with genuine reconciliation. They confront Judaism with an appreciative attitude that goes far beyond the condescensions of tolerance. Whereas so many

Christian theologians of past generations struggled to disentangle Christianity from its Jewish roots, contemporary Christian thinkers celebrate them. They speak in terms of the Judeo-Christian tradition, by which they mean certain theoretical formulations regarding God, man, and history, as well as a set of moral concerns.

In light of the tragic history of the Jews in Christian Europe, it is not surprising that many Jewish thinkers have approached the dialogue gingerly. In the call to the open confrontation of genuine dialogue they fear overtones of that ancient summons to conversion. In the new-found Christian enthusiasm for the "Old Testament" world-view they are afraid that they confront a mere change of tactics. They suspect that Christians are out to gain by flattery what they failed to gain by force: Jewish acknowledgment of the legitimacy of the Messianic claims made on behalf of Jesus of Nazareth. However, even Jewish thinkers who are convinced of the good will of Christian thinkers are nervous about dialogue. They fear that theological discussions with Christians are bound to lead Jewish participants into fundamental distortions of Judaism. As noted earlier, Christianity is a faith, whereas Judaism is a faith-people. The intellectual energies of Christian thinkers have traditionally been expended in theology, that is, in the effort to make its central doctrines intellectually coherent and philosophically persuasive. By contrast, Jewish thinkers have taken the theological foundations of Judaism for granted. Traditionally, they have expended their efforts on the study of Torah, that is, on the elaboration and codification of the sacred legislation of the Mosaic books. However, once theological discussions with Christians are launched, the pressures of communication lead Jewish participants to minimize this difference and to conform their tradition to the Christian pattern.

Yet, as Nathan Glazer has observed, there are internal pressures that have led the religious thinkers of American Judaism to change the traditional pattern by working hard at theology. In the ghettos of Europe the community was forced to cohere, and it was relatively isolated. Under these conditions the restriction of intellectual activity to the Talmudic tradition of legal interpretation was a source of strength; it provided both sacred authority and specific laws. In the United States today this pattern is ruinous. Here the major challenges to Judaism are intellectual. There is no possibility of securing the adherence of Jews to specific sacred laws if they do not accept their divine authority. In this context, concern for the theological underpinnings of the community are an inescapable responsibility of Jewish thinkers. It is obvious that this responsibility can be discharged more fruitfully if Jewish thinkers discuss the major issues with Christian theologians. Self-encapsulation has never been a creative policy in intellectual affairs.

These historical factors have made serious theological exchanges between Jews and Christians possible. To the limited extent that they have been successful they have broken down parochialism and stimulated reflection. Christian theologians cannot help benefiting from discussions of Abraham Heschel's views of prophecy, and Jewish thinkers gain a deeper understanding of the mean-

ing of Israel from Karl Barth's views of covenant.
On matters of this kind, the perspectives of Jews
and Christians may differ radically, but they share
the tools and excitement of a common intellectual
discipline. Indeed, the Jewish-Christian interchanges have actually led each tradition to engage
in new intellectual disciplines. Jewish thinkers,
apart from the Orthodox party, have followed
Protestant patterns of studying the Bible by means
of the techniques of modern literary and historical
research. On the other hand, Christian scholars
are increasingly aware of the need to master
Talmudic sources if they are to understand the
teachings of Jesus.

These limited gains in intellectual cooperation
and illumination are all that can be reasonably
expected of discussions between Jews and Christians. They will continue simply because they are
beneficial to both parties; but they will also continue to be tense, because the tragic conflicts of
history are not easily overcome. Neither guilt nor
sentimentality can bridge the irreconcilable differences that pivot around Jewish and Christian re-
sponses to the figure of Nazareth. In an extraordinary talk to a Christian audience, Martin Buber
once captured both the nature of these differences
and the hope for genuine confrontation that take
place in and through them. Buber noted that the
Christian regards the Jew as an incomprehensibly
obdurate man who refuses to acknowledge that in
Jesus of Nazareth God has offered redemption to
the world in a unique way. To the Jew, the Christian is the incomprehensibly daring man who can
look at the terrible state of the world and nevertheless affirm that, in some decisive way, its re-

demption has been accomplished. In the face of this gulf that divides the communities Buber affirmed that

It behooves both you and us to hold inviolably fast to our own true faith, that is, to our own deepest relation to truth. It behooves both of us to show a religious respect for the true faith of the other. This is not what is called "tolerance," our task is not to tolerate each other's waywardness but to acknowledge the real relationship in which both stand to the truth. Whenever we both, Christian and Jew, care more for God Himself than for our images of God, we are united in the feeling that our Father's house is differently constructed than our human models take it to be.

[1] It should, however, be noted that some of them have. See the advertisements in *The New York Times* of June 4th and June 23rd, 1967.

[2] "Communications," *Judaism,* Summer 1967, p. 363.

ISRAEL
THE MODERN STATE
AND CONTEMPORARY
JEWISH POINTS
OF VIEW

Balfour Brickner

I shall treat this topic in two sections: first, a brief review of varying Jewish ideological approaches to the idea of a modern state; and second, an attempt to analyze these approaches.

Since we are dealing with contemporary Jewish viewpoints, the beginning of the twentieth century is a convenient and descriptive starting point. It is appropriate because 1897 was the date of the first Zionist congress in Basle, Switzerland; because 1904 marks the date of Herzl's premature death and the growth of varying Zionist-nationalist ideologies; and because the ensuing fifty years were the most creative, most controversial, most demanding years in the history of Zionism, culminating in the creation of the modern state.

Professor Ben Halperin astutely observes (in *The Idea of the Jewish State*) that the goal of Zionism was not simply nationalistic, though to be sure it contained nationalistic elements: land, language, political sovereignty and a consciousness rooted in a remembered common past. Zionism dealt with a goal no other nationalism dealt with; the survival of a Jewish people whose security was seriously jeopardized by an anti-Semitism in the diaspora, against which the Jew could not effectively defend or assert himself.

A second distinguishing characteristic of Zionism was the fact that political sovereignty was not an absolute or unconditional purpose of the movement, though there was never a time when some Zionists did not somewhere in some way hold that idea as paramount. Most Zionists did not value national sovereignty for its own sake. They saw it as an instrument needed to obtain other ends in the nationalist movement: the freeing of Jews from countries of their oppression and the bringing of them to a new country even before that country exercised political sovereignty.

I

The plight of the Jews, their civic disabilities, economic restrictions, social oppression and popular hatred became clear to Theodore Herzl, an assimilated Viennese Jew, as he covered the Dreyfus trial in Paris. He emerged from that trial aware not only of the virulence and depth of anti-Semitism but also of his Jewish self and the fact that despite his affluent, secure, un-Jewish Viennese upbringing, he could have no home anywhere that was not a self-determined(ing) Jewish home(land).

His contemporary and critic Achad Ha Am (Asher Ginsberg, 1856–1927) had a different view of the need for the contemporary state. He emphasized, in addition to the problem of the Jews, the problem of Judaism. What he as a modern man found most intolerable in the Jewish situation was the eroding of the agreement among Jews as to their common peoplehood, the result of a loss of faith among the "enlightened" and the apparent irrelevance of orthodoxy to modern conditions.

Achad Ha Am Zionists, called Cultural Zionists, saw as the immediate goal of nationalism the revival of "secular Jewish culture" through the medium of the Hebrew language and through this the reestablishment of a minimal basis for consensus among the Jewish people. Hebrew would be the motivating bond, prerequisite for pursuing other nationalist aims. Language served the purpose of Jewish culture and not vice versa. Jewish culture had first to be revived before there could be any resettlement in Israel under conditions of political sovereignty or autonomy.

This, in Achad Ha Am's view, would be done by a relatively small, devoted nucleus that would constitute a soundly based, well-rooted Jewish society in Palestine. Only *after* the Jewish people had been rejuvenated and invigorated by its revived culture could it undertake the long historic task of resettling en masse in Palestine and thus reclaim its sovereignty. From such a hub, the lifegiving force would go out to the diaspora like rays from a sun, consolidating in that diaspora the cultural influence of the nucleus.

Achad Ha Am's Cultural Zionism did not predominate, for it was on the one hand too intellectual and on the other too Judaically demanding. Only now are Jews beginning to see its virtues and to reevaluate the state in light of its preachments. Conditions could not wait for Achad Ha Am. "The problem of Judaism" became a luxury, second in importance to the pressing "problems of the Jews"; the need for immediate mass migration to escape the by then ubiquitous European plague of anti-Semitism. This problem demanded a single solution, a territory—Palestine—where Jews could concentrate as a majority and exercise national sovereignty. Beyond that unity of agreement the Zionist movement split into two camps; one supported Herzl's views, holding that before Jews could go to Palestine in masses, the world Jewish community must establish the Jewish claim to sovereignty; the other believed that the first task of the Jew was to *settle* the land, for only on the basis of effective occupation could the claim of sovereignty be sustained. While "the establishment Zionists" implored the Turks, to no avail, for permission to immigrate to Palestine (then part of the Ottoman Empire) and resettle, a small band of Eastern European Jews, mostly from Russia, formed themselves into an activist movement known as BILU (from the first letters of four Hebrew words taken from the Psalms which in translation mean "O House of Jacob, come let us go up . . .") and in the 1880's made the first "aliyah" (migration) to Palestine.

The Basle program, adopted by the first Zionist Congress of 1897, reflected a compromise formula. The first sentence of that program declared the Zionist aim to be "the establishment of a home for the Jewish people secured under public law in Palestine." Further provisions reflected such other objectives as the "appropriate" resettlement of Palestine by Jewish farmers, artisans and entrepreneurs.

As negotiations for a legal charter for Palestine continuously floundered on the rocks of international political intrigue, the thrust of Zionism shifted to the establishment of projects or actual colonization under whatever legal conditions could be obtained at the time. It was not until the Balfour Declaration (November 1, 1917) and the Jewish national home clauses in the Palestine Mandate, following World War I, that the long sought for legal claims, which Herzl had set as Zionism's first aim, were realized. Balfour was then the British Foreign Secretary. His declaration stating that "His Majesty's government views with favor the establishment in Palestine of a national home for the Jewish people . . ." was promptly ratified by the United States and by the governments of France and Italy. By this time more than 100,000 Jews lived in Palestine.

The history of Zionism during the 1920's was the story of debate between the "practical Zionists," now champions of Herzl's idea of "a home for the Jewish people secured under public law in Palestine," and the "Revisionists," who argued for "a Jewish state within its historic boundaries," including Transjordan.

Until 1920, Arab hostility to Jewish national independence had not crystalized. To the contrary, at the Paris Peace Conference, Emir Faisal, spokesman for the Arab kingdom of Hedjaz (later to become Jordan), announced full acceptance of the Balfour Declaration.

By this time the redoubtable Chaim Weizmann had become the leading figure in the Zionist movement. Unlike either Herzl or the Revisionist, Jabotinsky, Weizmann saw as central the gradual building up of the Yishuv (the Jewish settlement) on sound social, cultural and economic foundations, against the time when the political future of the country would have to be finally determined. He vigorously opposed any and all discussion that forced issues of political sovereignty. "As carefully, he nurtured every grain of autonomy of political organization of the Jewish community itself; an independent school system, a self defense corps (later to become the Hagganah), institutions of self-government and above all the slowly growing network of agricultural settlements."

During the 1930's three factors unified and galvanized contemporary Jewish thinking:

1. Revisions in the American immigration laws of the 1920's, which effectively barred Jews (as well as other Eastern and Southern Europeans) from entering America.

2. Britain's incredible behavior in Palestine as Mandatory Power, culminating in the "White Paper of 1939," by which Jews were allowed to buy land in only five percent of Palestine and that in an area where Jews were most thickly settled, and then restricting the number of Jewish immigrants to Palestine to a maximum of 75,000 over a period of five years, after which all Jewish immigration was to cease.

3. The rise of Hitler and the obvious end of the European Jewish community.

The reaction to these events led to the famous Biltmore Formula of 1942 (named for the Biltmore Hotel, New York City, where it was formulated by leaders, primarily of American Zionism, in conference assembled). This platform first denounced the 1939 White Paper "as a breach and a repudiation of the Balfour Declaration." Secondly, it called for the fulfillment of the underlying purpose of the Mandate for Palestine—the establishment of a Jewish Commonwealth. It demanded that full powers to achieve this aim be delegated to the Jewish Agency for Palestine; in other words it demanded that all power for the development of the country pass into the hands of the autonomous institutions of the world Jewish community. That demand was only six years premature, not long, when one remembers that the power had been sought in prayer, in song, in hope for over 2,000 years. Six years later the demand became a reality.

Today there are many who, knowing little or nothing about the history of the Middle East, and accepting only the propagandistic half truths presented by both Israel and Arab partisans, think that the Jewish community has been consistently insensitive to Arab claims and demands. Nothing could be more unrealistic. In the world of contemporary Zionism, the majority of Zionists were prepared to establish a Jewish state in only part of Palestine, recognizing the existence of an Arab state in the other. The concept was known as bi-nationalism. In the 1930's and 1940's bi-nationalism as a solution was seriously proposed by Zionists sensitive to the need for obtaining Arab consent to the form (not the question) of statehood that should ultimately obtain in and for Palestine. Many hoped that Britain and the world community would impose on both Jews and Arabs this bi-national solution. Britain, however, showed no inclination to come forward with solutions that ran the risk of opposition and rejection by either or both parties to the disputed and growing claims to sovereignty. Thus, the opportunity for diplomacy was missed and in its place there emerged

incredible efforts to limit and restrict the Yishuv.
This was met with political opposition and physical resistance. And yet, despite the Jewish passion
inflamed by the British blockade of ships carrying
the refuged refuse of the concentration camps,
and despite Britain's intolerable behavior, the majority of Zionists continued to reject any idea of
seeking to overthrow British mandatory rule by
armed uprising as practiced by the Stern gang
and the Irgun Discussion. Legal, political and
moral pressure, not recourse to arms, were the
ways Zionists chose to fulfill their ideals. By 1942,
those responsible for the direction of Zionism
knew that the east bank, Transjordan, was no
longer an option to be considered for the Jewish
state. Jews could claim only what they occupied.
Weizmann had been right. By 1942, an area of
Jewish settlement that was at least conceivable
as a viable state had begun to take shape (on the
west bank). Palestine was now a defensible if not
desirable alternative to the nominal goals of the
Biltmore program. By the time the British Labor
government came to power, it became quite obvious that if Jews were to receive any state at all
in Palestine, it would be a partitioned one—not
the one dreamed of by Herzl or Jabotinsky.

The State of Israel was voted into existence by
the General Assembly of the United Nations on
November 29, 1947. The vote was 33 to 13. The
state finally established was less than 8,000 square
miles—out of the 45,000 originally conceived by
the Balfour plan—and this in one small corner of
an Arab world that stretched 3,533,107 square
miles. Within 24 hours, Arab armies began "the
Jihad that failed." Israel survived.

II

Are all Jews Zionists? Were all Jews avid supporters of the varying proposals for the establishment of a Jewish state? Opposition to Zionism came from such diametrically opposing quarters as the American Council for Judaism and the ultra-Orthodox Agudat Israel. That is all they share in common. To this day, these organizations continue to carry on a niggling, "shin-nipping" kind of campaign, the major thrust of which can obviously no longer be opposition to the creation of the State of Israel, or even to recognition of that state, but a kind of imperial disassociation from what the state does, picking at its flaws and seeking to demonstrate that one's Judaism is not necessarily tied to one's recognition of Israel.

The voice of the American Council for Judaism is much louder than it is effective. It represents such a miniscule part of the Jewish people that the rest of Jewry has a tendency to dismiss its words and arguments as completely unreal and irrelevant. Here in the American corner of the diaspora neither the Council nor the ultra-Orthodox have any political power or sociological clout whatsoever. They can be dismissed with impunity.

In Israel, however, where for obvious reasons the American Council for Judaism cannot and does not exist, the ultra-Orthodox do constitute a bloc with which the government and the populace must reckon, particularly in places like Jerusalem where the majority of their members dwell in the ghettoized isolation of the Mea Shaarim quarter. There they cannot be so easily dismissed, for on various occasions and under certain circumstances, they can and do create conditions of civil disturbance. Paradoxically, their continued safety and the security of their right *not* to recognize the existence of the State of Israel, because it was brought into being by secular powers and not by the advent of the Messiah, is possible only as the state exists to protect their insistence that the state ought not to exist.

Having now "confessed" what you all know—that not all Jews are either Zionists or even "lovers of Zion"—let me hastily add that in my judgment the vast majority, at least of American Jews, most certainly are, if not actual Zionists, surely men and women who see enormous practical value and spiritual significance in the State of Israel, who either actively supported or passively tolerated its struggle for birth as already outlined and who are overwhelmingly committed to its continued existence. Thus, when it was threatened with annihilation, as most Jews in the world thought it was in June 1967, it was neither strange nor surprising to see world Jewry massively rise up to support the state's right to exist. By threatening to attack Israel, Nasser unknowingly threatened the Jews' very identity.

Identity is only the name we give to a collective social ego. Remove a man's ego and you destroy him as a man. Rob a person of his identity and you destroy his ego, his ability to say to himself and others: "This is what and who I am." Translated into the language of Jewish identity, it sounds something like this: "All right, I may not believe in God. I am not a member of any Jewish race. That is an outworn, false concept anyway. Jews are not a race. I am a citizen of the country to which I have political allegiance. I admire Israel and the Israeli. So what? So do lots of non-Jews. What am I? I am a Jew. I do not know exactly what that means and really don't care, until someone curses me with the name or tries to take Israel from the Jewish people. Then I become aware of its presence in my life, and my equally indefinable relationship to it. Then I become aware of the fact that place and people are somehow intertwined. The place gave birth to those historic memories that in part make me as a Jew whatever I am so long as I choose to be self-identified by that word or permit others so to identify me."

The writer Eli Weisel expressed this feeling quite accurately when, after a visit to the Wailing Wall last June, he wrote:

The war has compelled each Jew to confront his people, his past and his God. I try to understand, to believe—I succeed a bit . . . but the truth is, I still don't understand. The more the professional experts try to explain, the less I understand. It all seems like an ancient legend as though we had all gone far, far back to the past. Perhaps that's why I have an almost palpable feeling of victory—we have conquered time itself? And our generation is not privileged to boast many such victories.

This generally describes the way most (and by that I mean the overwhelming number of) Jews in America feel about Israel and their relationship to it. The fact that so many emptied their pocketbooks and in other ways gave of themselves, when Israel's very existence seemed cruelly threatened, only confirms my belief that this is indeed an

accurate description. Has it always been so, at
least in the contemporary world? Have the majority of Jews always shared this passion? Neither
Theodore Herzl nor his practical Zionism were
popular ideologies with the leaders of Western
Jewry: Baron de Hirsch, the Rothschilds and the
others. His theories *were* popular with the people
—those already *fevered* with the desire to resettle
Palestine and to colonize it under formally established, adequate, recognized legal rights. With
them he won the day at the Basle Congress. Thus
he was able to confide in his diary of that historic
first meeting: "In Basle, I founded the Jewish
state. If I said that aloud today, I would be met
by universal laughter. Perhaps, in five years, certainly in fifty, everyone will see it." But "every
new idea necessarily calls forth a division," and it
did not take long for those divisions to appear
even among elements of the Jewish community
committed to the restoration of Zion.

In principle, of course, those (predominantly
German, classically Reform) Jews, who cham-
pioned the idea of emancipation and integration
into the total society, rejected Zionism and Zionism
rejected them. The ideological rejection was complicated by an East-West split within Jewry. Jews
of middle Europe looked with disdain on their
eastern European brothers, whom they characterized as generally uneducated, uncultured, totally
ghettoized, steeped only in their own internal
parochial orthodoxy. Eastern European Jewry had
an equally pejorative view of their Western cou-
sins, whom they characterized as assimilationist,
un-Jewish Jews. To suggest to a westernized German Jew that his homeland was Jerusalem and

not Berlin or that his mother tongue was to be
Hebrew rather than German was as theologically
heretical as it was practically unsound. Thus, in
July 1897, the classic formulation of anti-Zionism
was expressed by the "Protest Rabbis" (all German) who said in a press release:

The efforts of so called Zionists to found a Jewish
national state in Palestine contradict the Messianic
promises of Judaism as contained in the Holy Writ
and in later religious sources, Judaism obligates its
adherents to serve with all devotion the Fatherland
to which they belong and to further its national interests with all their heart and with all their strength.
However, those noble aims directed toward the
colonization of Palestine by Jewish peasants and
farmers are not in contradiction to these obligations,
because they have no relation whatsoever to the
founding of a national state.

Little wonder also that Reform Judaism in
America, whose origins and roots were German,
became until the second half of the twentieth century the classic resting place of the anti-Zionist
viewpoint. It is not surprising to read the following in the Pittsburgh platform of 1895 blueprint
for classic reform:

We consider ourselves no longer a nation, but a
religious community, and therefore expect neither a
return to Palestine nor a sacrificial worship under the
administration of the sons of Aaron, nor the restoration of any of the laws concerning the Jewish state.

It was not until 1937 and after the bitterest of
ideological battles that Reform Judaism officially

changed its attitude. This change is incorporated in the words of the Columbus Platform of the Central Conference of American Rabbis.

Judaism is the soul of which Israel is the living body. . . . In the rehabilitation of Palestine, the land hallowed by memories and hopes, we behold the promise of renewed life for many of our brethren. We affirm the obligation of all Jewry to aid in the upbuilding as a Jewish homeland by endeavoring to make it not only a haven of refuge for the oppressed but also a center of Jewish culture and spiritual life.

Anti-Zionism also took on the form of opposition to the colonizing of Palestine as the only home for the Jewish people in preference to other possible colonization sites, i.e., Mesopotamia or Uganda, both of which were at one time offered to Herzl. There were Zionists who saw in the practical difficulties of securing legal rights to Palestine from the Sultan the danger of losing the lives of many eastern European Jews, who because of Czarist persecutions (for example, the Kishineff pogrom of 1903) simply had to leave Russia and other eastern European lands. Listen to Herzl at the Sixth Zionist Congress in 1903:

. . . Palestine is the one land where our people can come to rest. But hundreds of thousands are waiting for immediate help. There is only one way of resolving this contradiction; I must resign the leadership. I will, if you so desire, conduct the next Congress; after that, elect two action committees; one for East Africa and one for Palestine. . . .

The Uganda proposal split the Zionist movement. One of the strongest advocates urging an alternative for Palestine was the eloquent and distinguished British writer, Israel Zangwill. The entire idea enjoyed the cooperation of Western Jews and a movement was formed called Jewish Territorial Organization (ITO). Indeed it attracted the support of many outstanding non-territorialist Jews, including such well-known American Jews as Oscar S. Straus, Daniel Guggenheim and Judge Mayer Sulzberger. Even Jacob H. Schiff was attracted to it. It led eventually to his Galveston Project, whereby a small number of Russian Jews were settled in the interior of America on the theory that hostility to the Jews as a minority group was directly related to their numbers and concentration. Remove them from the ghettos of the eastern seaboard and you remove one of the major causes of anti-Semitism.

For nine years Zangwill sought in vain for a charter to found an autonomous Jewish colony somewhere in the world. World War I put an end to ITO, and with the subsequent Balfour Declaration gave renewed impetus to the main dream of Zionism—settlement in Palestine and no other place.

The Balfour Declaration and the establishment of the British Mandate in Palestine converted some of the ideological premises of Zionism into internationally recognized legal provisions. The next twenty years were marked by the ebb and flow of internal political and ideological disputes, disenchantment with the British Mandate power and militant hostility in Palestine by an aroused Arab populace. Over all, of course, hung the rising shadow of the Nazi swastika. Through it all the bulk of the Jewish people remained faithful to the dream of a Jewish state in Palestine, though the "how" and "when" remained a gossamer-like vision. In the West, Zionism slowly acquired a favorable climate of opinion and a network of institutional support drawing in the entire community through channels that sometimes called themselves non-Zionist. In the year following the adoption of the Biltmore Platform, American Zionism experienced a threefold increase in its registered membership, reaching almost half a million. Public opinion polls conducted in 1945 showed that the attitudes of the Jews in America were strongly favorable to the idea of a Jewish state, and Gentile opinion was also strongly sympathetic. A short-lived American Jewish Conference was formed, which adopted the demand for a Jewish commonwealth in Palestine. When the American Jewish Committee (up to that moment a non-Zionist organization, leaning slightly to anti-Zionism) left the conference, they did so as a dissident minority.

But the two factors most responsible for converting Western non-Zionism into Zionism were the horror of the holocaust and the fact that the world's governments began to conclude that the partition of Palestine was the only rational and feasible solution to the difficulties of that area. On November 29, 1947, the General Assembly of the United Nations adopted a United Nations Special Committee to Palestine proposal to partition Palestine into Jewish and Arab states.

Behind the unbounded Jewish joy lay a realization on the part of diaspora Zionists that their roles had become radically transformed as a result of their crowning success. As for the Israelis, they too were now confronted with the problem of formulating the nature of their relationship to the diaspora Jewish community where the majority of Jews live—not in *galut,* not in exile, but in diaspora.

The two communities, Israel and the diaspora, have had little more than twenty years of experience with one another. These two decades have not always been harmonious. After the initial halcyon days of rejoicing in the fulfillment of an age-old dream, the realities of "the marriage" set in. I speak not of the attitude of the American Council for Judaism, which states that it is not legitimate for the American Jewish community to manifest a sympathetic interest in the State of Israel. The council distinguishes sharply between the state and the Jewish religious community in Israel, recognizing as natural only an interest in the latter and imputing a taint of disloyalty to Jews who express their natural sympathy for the former through political and/or cultural channels. It is indeed a fringe philosophy of a fringe group. (They claim a membership of 20,000, though it is probably not half that in actuality). No, I speak of the hundreds of thousands, perhaps millions, of American Jews who are troubled by the realization that there is a serious danger that Israel and the diaspora may be drifting apart—a drift which to be sure the Six Day War halted, if only temporarily. An amazingly perceptive article in the June issue of the Catholic publication, *Herder Correspondence,* reflects with probing insight the attitudes of many American Jews to a non-war threatened Israel: "What the Jew abroad wants from Israel is precisely what it had no present in-

tention or possibility of becoming: a fully organized and working Judaism, and not merely an
Israeli state with military and financial preoccupa-
tions. The great majority of Israelis have no in-
tention of adopting Judaism in practice."

There was a mental gap between the diaspora
Jew visiting Israel and returning disappointed
(having seen prosperity but not Judaism) and the
young Israeli whom he met there—blatantly and
openly anti-Judaistic (as he identified *it* with the
observance of traditional liturgies and rituals),
persuaded that the axis of the world bisected
Jerusalem and that the entire world rotated around
it. "Why don't you come to live in Israel?" is now
a jingoistic slogan, said by Sabras as much out of
bluster as out of nationalism. It may be that Israel,
being an essentially Jewish (at least non-Christian) culture, affords the Jew the luxury of repu-
diating his Judaic (religious) self without repudi-
ating his Jewish (ethnic) self and to do this
without fear of criticism from an outside, osten-
sibly Christian world.

No discussion of contemporary Jewish points
of view about Israel can fail to point out the
convolutions that so many so-called Jewish intel-
lectuals are now undergoing as a result of the new
image of the Jew: as a "tough as nails" fighter
farmer, determined, at time pitiless, both militarily
efficient and maddeningly makeshift, who always
gets the job done and who always wins. What a
difference this is from the image that Raul Hilberg
and Hannah Arendt would paint for us—the Jews
going like docile sheep to the slaughter they somehow already knew awaited them. In my judgment, Robert Alter is quite correct when (*Com-*

mentary, October 1967) he accuses intellectual Jews like I. F. Stone of moral schizophrenia, unable to resolve their own uneasiness except by directing a qualified hostility toward Israel. They are, he suggests, either out of touch with the fact of an increasing sense of unity between Israelis and Jews around the world, or what is worse, they either deny or distort the fact that in each of the three Israeli-Arab wars, both Israel's territory and the number of Arab homeless grew.

There are even those in the Jewish intelligentsia camp ranging far to the left who hew close to the Moscow line on the Middle East—that Israel was created by Western imperialism to be a buffer and irritant and that the Israeli attack on the Arabs was "a Pearl Harbor," backed by the West. The trouble with this line of reasoning is that those who advance it forget that Arabs have not won a war in the past thousand years, and that their own military stupidity, such as digging their tanks into the sand, following the instructions of a Russian military manual designed for other climes, condemn them more than anything that can be said to the contrary. But above all other faults, what the Jewish intelligentsia with their broad universalistic, humanistic, usually Jewishly self-hating view of things fail to understand, and what the Jewish people understand so easily and so completely, is that lofty visions of universalism with no roots sunk into the soil of natural identity is as impossible as it is undesirable. Men must belong to a particular part of mankind before trying to embrace the whole of it. As Alter writes: "Israel's very presence among the nations is an affirmation that the Jews are not symbols, witnesses, ghostly emissaries of some obscure mission, but men like other men, who need to occupy physical space in a real world before they can fulfill whatever loftier aspirations they may have." And I might add, Jews throughout the world are bound and determined that this situation, presently existing, shall continue.

ISRAEL
THE MODERN STATE:
AND CONTEMPORARY
CHRISTIAN POINTS
OF VIEW

Phillip Scharper

We had a ball. The Jewish-Christian dance was beyond everyone's expectations. We became accustomed to each other's music—and even came to like it. We got to know each other's style and could waltz or Watusi without worrying about our partner. Even the wallflowers seemed at the point of swinging onto the floor.

Then the bombs fell, and we could hear the dull krumpf of mortars in the distance. The music stopped in mid-note; we gazed at each other and realized that each seemed to be gazing at a stranger. And in many cases—we were. Why? Why would the Jew in particular now see, in the face of many a Christian, incomprehension or suspicion where previously he thought he had seen understanding or even affection?

Sources of Strain

There are, of course, many reasons. Life rarely gives us the luxury of a single explanation for the breakdown of human relationships. The strains placed upon Jewish-Christian understanding by the June War came from many sources, most of which had little to do with the war itself. We shall deal with only three.

1. Residual anti-Semitism. The Arab-Israeli war was the occasion (not the cause) for a measurable amount of Christian anti-Semitism to emerge from the underground caves to which it had been slowly driven over the past decade. Far from destroyed, it remained there, sullen but silent, until some dramatic world event would permit it to come to the surface with the appearance of respectability and responsibility.

Typical of this type of reaction, perhaps, are the statements of a well-known Christian religious educator who wrote:

The Jews are *the* enemy. The more they *appear* to be helpless victims, the more they are in actuality conspiring as the devil's own agents of destruction. Before the anti-Christ conquers the world, let us expose him for what he is.

2. The conviction that issues in the Mideast are too complex politically to permit moral or religious judgment. One must recognize the operation of prudence in this position. After all, only God and the pessimist are ever in full possession of the facts. Nevertheless, in the case of the Mideast, certain factors would seem clear enough not only to permit but to demand the moral response of the churches.

The fact that the threat of genocide was raised, not only throughout the spring of 1967 but over the years, should have evoked more than a shrug of the collective Christian shoulder. One cannot but wonder if the same response of no-response would have been given if the threat to annihilate the enemy had come from the Knesset and Tel-Aviv, before or during the period of armed conflict.

The question of control of Jerusalem is perhaps more gray, but not so gray that one cannot discern patches of color moving toward both black and white. I, for one, would not agree that "religious questions should not be raised before the political ones are solved." Jerusalem is a holy city in a deeper and broader sense than is any other city upon earth. Those voices—including the Vatican—that call for international control *now* were effectively silent when Jordan held the Old City and forbade the majority of Israeli Jews and Arabs to visit their holy places.

3. The Christian failure to see the Jewish state and the Jewish people as a theological fact that challenges the Christian. This particular Christian failure was given an almost classical expression by Dr. Willard Oxtoby:

Thus, while in the Christian's view the State of Israel is simply a political fact, for many Jews it is a profoundly religious fact. For many American Jews, Zionism functions as a defense against assimilation to modern secular culture. They have no particular interest in traditional theology and ritual observance, but their community can achieve a sense of meaning and relevance by sacrificing financially for Israel.

I would like to analyze the reasons for the third Christian view, because it seems to indicate a major reason why dialogue broke off in the spring —and why it was less than an authentic dialogue even before that time. Then, I would like to suggest a path Jews and Christians might follow together, after the broken bridges have been mended. At the risk, then, of seeming incredibly romantic as a theologian, I proceed.

We Christians seem, almost without exception, to have collectively but little understanding of the Jewish people into which Christ our Lord was born. It will not do, to allay this feeling, to refer in the Catholic context to either the statement on the Jews in the declaration of Vatican II nor to the paragraphs on the Jews in Pope Paul's encyclical *Ecclesiam Suam*. Nor will it do to refer to the statements that have issued, with all goodwill, from other major Christian communities.

In these Christian statements there seems to be a muted but nonetheless significant theme: the suggestion that, in the religious history of Western man, the Jew is to be found as an obdurate fact who has either, with characteristic perverseness, refused to die to corroborate our theology of the Jew, or who perdures only to serve as a reminder to us of God's graciousness in inviting us into the household of the Christian faith.

Nor is it enough to explain, as some sophisticated Christians are now validly explaining, the indebtedness of Christianity to the Old Testament, the need for the contemporary Christian to attempt to recover Hebraic thought patterns in order to understand his own spiritual heritage, or to trace the evolution of Christian liturgy from Jewish ritual forms. This type of Christian approach to Judaism only repeats, in more sophisticated modes, the general inadequacy of the Christian approach to Judaism—the assumption that the Jewish people have no valid history after the destruction of Jerusalem. It assumes that the only theological relationship of Christianity to Judaism must be to Judaism as the Christian understands it—a Judaism locked in the past—as though all of the spiritual energy of post-biblical Judaism had become a frozen waterfall, to sink its energy and beauty in the sand.

But it is with a living Judaism that the Christian is summoned to have dialogue today, and the contemporary Christian must recognize that he is to speak and listen to the contemporary Jew, who is no more exclusively a product of the Old Testament than is the Christian himself.

For the Jew, whether the Christian knows or cares, has a post-biblical history as long, obviously, as that of the Christian. There have been developments within Judaism since the diaspora, and these developments demand of the Christian that he approach the Jew not only in sociological or historical terms but also as a theological problem.

The nature of this theological problem can perhaps be crudely stated in halting phrases such as: What is the theological reason for the continuing existence of Judaism, the Old Israel? What are we to make, here and now, of Paul's statement that "the calls and promises of God to the people of Israel are irrevocable"? We Christians must take more seriously than we have the fact that the Old Israel, as well as the New, is the community of love shaped on the anvil of a divine calling, the work of the Spirit of God. As a consequence, we must attempt to realize what the Jew has been and done through the two thousand years of concomitant Christian history; more importantly, we must strive to discern the design of providence in the fact that after these two thousand years of a common history, the Old Israel and the New find themselves in a situation of coexistence, confrontation and now dialogue, despite the persecution, forced conversions and garroting with a silken thread which we Christians have historically visited upon the Jew, despite our proclamation that ours, too, is the God of Abraham, Isaac and Jacob.

But we must see this theological question as a living one, drawing its life from the stubborn soil of present reality. We cannot treat the theological question of the Jew as though it were an exotic one, hanging like a jungle orchid rootless in the heavy air. Part of the context in which the Christian must place the problem. is the historical experience of the Jew in our century. And part of that experience is the creation and existence of the State of Israel.

Am I completely wrong in thinking that for most Christians the State of Israel seems to be but a political reality, which therefore does not lure the Christian mind into theological speculation on its origin, continuance or ultimate purpose? I cannot, of course, speak for other Christians, or even justify theologically my own response to what I have seen in Israel. But I do think it worthy of remark that, as a Christian, I was reminded again and again in Israel of the ancient prophecy of Ezechiel when he saw the valley filled with dry bones restored to life at God's command:

Behold, O my people, I will open your graves, and cause you to come up out of your graves, and bring you into the land of Israel . . . and you shall live, and

I shall place you in your own land: then shall you
know that I the Lord have spoken it and performed
it.

As a single Christian, I could find in the fact and
the fortune of the State of Israel only a fulfillment
of the ancient prophecy. But twenty years ago,
six million Jews lay dead in Europe and the spared
but scattered remnant seemed, to the eyes of
human vision, helpless and perhaps doomed. Certainly, no Christian nation of the West was inviting *these* tempest-tossed to its shores, or lifting the
torch of hope above its golden door. Yet in that
time the State of Israel was born and the impossible took place. The dry bones stirred and were
clothed once more with flesh; the people were
summoned from their graves and were brought
into their own land. Was it indeed that the Lord
had spoken and performed it?

We Christians may not believe so but we must,
at least, try to understand why so many Jews both
within and without Israel look upon this state as
God's reply to a people's faith. We might also at
least strive to see, in the newly gathered Israel, an
analogy to the church as a sign raised up among
the nations to proclaim that God is faithful to his
promises and that the calls of God to the people
of Israel are "irrevocable."

What are we Christians to make, theologically,
of the yet more staggering experience of the Jew
within our own lifetime—the fact that more than
six million of their number met death for no other
crime than that they traced their origin to Jerusalem and Sinai and the land to which Abraham

was called—all features that claim prominent place in our own topography of the Spirit. It would be difficult for the Christian to find, even in his own churches of silence behind the Iron-Bamboo curtains, the experience of a religious community more reminiscent of Isaiah's depiction of the Suffering Servant; a people acquainted with grief and sorrow, dumb before their executioners and led like lambs to the slaughter.

Even if we discount all this and yet retain some vestige of belief in redemptive suffering, can we quite discount the possibility that hundreds of thousands of Jewish children in Dachau and Auschwitz may somehow have died for us, even as we traditionally honor those Jewish children of an earlier time, the Holy Innocents, whose death, violent and unsought, was yet seen as martyrdom by the eyes of Christian faith? May it be that by the stripes of these latter day Innocents we are healed, or at least have had the hope of healing proffered to us?

Ezechiel and Isaiah are, I suspect, very much on the mind and in the heart of the modern Jew as he approaches the contemporary dialogue with the Christian; we cannot, as a consequence, do him the dishonor of looking upon him, as he talks and listens to us, as less than a theological problem. We must try to understand why, for him, these places and moments of the twentieth century have not merely a social or political but a sacred significance. What I have been trying to say was said better by Karl Barth: "In order to be chosen we must, for good or ill, either be Jews or else be heart and soul on the side of the Jews."

The Ecumenism of Jew and Christian with the World

Jew and Christian alike must recognize their "pre-ecumenical" solidarity with the rest of mankind, with those who have a different faith or no faith in the accepted ecclesiastical understanding of that term. Before we are either Jew or Christian, we are human beings and members of the family of God the Father, shaped by his creating hand, called into being by his breath. Wherever we turn in either the Old or the New Testament, we are forced to confront not an anthropology but a religious understanding of man's origin and destiny. Since a divine origin and destiny are common to every man, his links to every other man are beyond his forging or his power to break.

Regardless of whether those who do not share this Judeo-Christian view of man recognize themselves as sons of God, we recognize them as such and can only speak of and to them as our brothers, whose dignity we have neither designed nor given, and with whose destiny we are not allowed to tamper.

Alike, the Jew and the Christian believe that, in the last sifting of reality, there is only one history, the record of God's continual breaking in upon the world of man and speaking to man through event, even as he spoke to Moses through the event of a bush that burned, yet was not consumed.

Neither Jew nor Christian has the right to put man-made limits to God's capacity to speak through events. We can only strive to hear what God may be saying through events, even in the events of this glorious but torn and tragic century.

What, for example, is God trying to say to us—Jew and Christian—through this event: that we comprise, in the white Western community, less than one-third of the world's peoples and yet consume more than 60 percent of the world's goods, and control more than 70 percent of the world's resources? What do we make of this event: that the world has shrunken to the dimensions of a village, and that in this village we live in the houses set upon the hill, moated from our fellow-villagers by green and spacious lawns, scandalously conspicuous in our expenditure on luxuries and our waste of necessities? What do we make of this event: that the number of villagers who are non-white, non-Jewish, non-Christian, is increasing rapidly to the point where, by the year 2000, we will be an even smaller minority than we are at the moment, for that will be a world wherein the population of China alone may number 1,700,000,000—400,000,000 more than the present population of Europe, North and South America, the Soviet Union and Africa combined.

What is God saying to us through these events? Is he not trying to say that we must learn from one another and teach our children that, in the world they will inherit, they must be the conscious heirs of all that is most authentic in what we call, somewhat too glibly, the Judeo-Christian tradition? We must attempt to become now, and hope that our children will be in the future, the *anawim* —the poor of God—open constantly to the breathing of his Spirit. This much, at least, we can hope to do together, if we make the effort to understand who we are and who the other is; we can attempt to show the emerging world—brown, black, illiterate, impoverished—that we are indeed their brothers, for each of us holds dear the ancient words of Isaiah:

> The Spirit of the Lord is upon me,
> because he has anointed me
> To bring good news to the poor; he has sent
> me to proclaim to the captives release,
> and sight to the blind;
> To set at liberty the oppressed;
> to proclaim the acceptable year of the
> Lord, and the day of recompense.

To suggest that we who are divided in creed might yet be united in deed is of course to suggest a complete reversal of so many of our long-held and deeply cherished attitudes and convictions. But this is *kairos,* the acceptable time of the Lord, and even *chronos* tells us that there is little time left. Why can we not speak with one voice against the palpable injustices within our own society, and move with one heart toward the healing of the wounds of mankind—our family and God's—throughout the world. It may well be that church and synagogue must strip itself of many of its own possessions, and relinquish something of its smug righteousness, in order to show in our actions the compassion of the God in whom our brother does not believe.

Visionary? Perhaps. But our very being here through these days would have seemed visionary less than a decade ago. Impossible? Not to the *anawim,* the little ones of God who were yet great: an Abraham, a Moses, a Mary of Nazareth who knew that the surest sign of God's power was man's native incapacity to accomplish God's design. For the *anawim* of our age must come to know what the *anawim* have always known—that only he who can see the invisible can accomplish the impossible.

A CHRISTIAN UNDERSTANDING OF THE ELECTION OF ISRAEL

Frank M. Cross, Jr.

In his own self-understanding, the Christian devises his doctrine of the election of Israel from the Bible, from the law and history and oracles of the Hebrew Bible and from the gospels and epistles of the Greek Bible. He expounds his doctrine on the ground of scripture alone and first of all from the plain or historical meaning thereof. This may come as a surprise to the sociologist who examines Christian attitudes toward the Jews, and perhaps it will appear preposterous to the Jewish historian who examines Jewish-Christian relationships of the past. Nevertheless the major churches in Christendom necessarily conform their theological teaching on the election of the Jews to biblical doctrine as best understood in the biblical interpretation of their age. This is obviously true of the churches of the magisterial Reformation, the Reformed and Lutheran churches; it is also true increasingly of the Roman Catholic Church, whose leading present-day theologians join their Protestant brethren in proclaiming the principle of *sola scriptura*.

1. Our first task therefore is to sketch the biblical doctrine of the vocation of Israel according to contemporary Christian exegesis.

Our earliest extensive work recoverable in the
Hebrew Bible is the old Israelite Epic, a work first
precipitated into prose form in the era of the
Israelite empire. One may describe it as expressing
the exuberance and faith of Davidic Israel. The
Epic in its Yahwistic variant may even be described as the central document of the biblical
faith, its first normative statement. In Israel the
literary epic became the primary religious form,
replacing the mythic cycle of the pagan cultus.

The Israelite Epic interprets history as a drama
of divine works of salvation. Israel's history is cast
over against the background of universal history.
The key to universal history is seen in two parallel
accounts of human rebellion: man's attempt to become like a god, and the tale of the social revolt
of mankind, revealed in the pretensions of the
state symbolized by Babel, the city, and its tem-
ple-tower lifting toward heaven. Universal history
narrows to the epic of God's dealings with Israel,
which must somehow be understood as having,
therefore, universal significance. The *magnalia
dei,* performed in Israel's midst, provide a means
to overcome human alienation and point ultimately to the divine victory in history and to the establishment of the divine rule over the human community.

The *locus classicus* relating to Israel's calling in
the Epic source is found in Genesis 12:1-3. From
the fall of society in chapter 11, we move to the
present age and the call of Abraham in chapter 12.

Go out from your land and kindred, and from thy
father's house, to the land I shall show thee. I shall
make of thee a great nation, and I shall bless thee,
and I shall make thy name great. Be thou a blessing,

and I shall bless those who bless you and curse those
who curse you. All the families of the earth will seek
blessing for themselves in thee. (Genesis 12:1-3; cf.
Jeremiah 4:2)

This is but one of a cycle of Epic passages bearing the theme, "promises to the patriarch." Indeed
the mass of tradition in the Epic is structured by
the theme of "promises" on the one hand, and on
the other hand by the fulfillment of these promises
in the creation of the nation Israel in the deliverance from Egypt, the gift of the land in conquest
and the gift of the covenant at Sinai. In other
words, we find here the characteristic repetition of
epic; the adumbration of election and the establishment of the chosen people.

The ultimate meaning of Israel's vocation is not
fully or plainly spelled out. This would become
clear in the Exile. We note, however, the reiter-
ated insistence that somehow the blessing and
curse, the weal and woe, of the nations is bound
up with Israel's call. That the calling of Israel is
thrown against a universal past also suggests that
we should project the significance of the events of
Israel's history against a universal future. The
mystery of the significance of Israel's calling is also
alluded to in another passage whose parallelistic
form suggests its origin in poetic epic:

> Thus you shall say to the house of Jacob,
> and announce to the children of Israel:
> You have seen what I have done to Egypt,
> and that I lifted you up on eagles' wings,
> and brought you to myself.
> Now, if you carefully hearken to my voice
> and keep my covenant,

> Then you will become my special possession
> among all the nations, for the whole earth is
>   mine.
> You shall become a nation of priests to me
> and a holy people.   (Exodus 19:3b-6a)

In exile, the community of Jews faced a crisis in their traditional faith in Israel's election and vocation. God had abandoned her in her sin, and invoked the curses of the violated covenant.

The edition of the Deuteronomic history completed in the Exile recast Israel's history of redemption. History was to be understood as the record of Israel's disobedience and the curses of the covenant, intertwined with intervals of obedience and divine blessing. God's ancient promises were cancelled, and the new hope in the election of the house of David was shattered. Exile was the end, though God might again listen to the prayers of the repentant in exile.

These views were intolerable to the faithful. The author of the dialogues of Job repudiated a historical faith that saw a direct and simple correlation between suffering and sin, piety and blessing. The book of Job is more radical than later traditionalists understood and it has suffered much corruption. Nevertheless it is clear that Job repudiates the older theologies of history. Israel's god, the free sovereign of history, is hidden from Job's eyes. Job cannot discern God's justice or power in the history he knows. In exile the God of history disappeared. Only the transcendent God of creation, El or Ba'l, lord of nature, appeared in the storm to speak to Job. In some quarters we have heard an echo of Job's harangue: that the God of history died at Auschwitz. We must seek new reconcilation with the gods of the land, we must attend to the myths of the psyche.

This was not the direction Israel was to take. A new tradition emerged from the agonies of the Exile, which affirmed the sovereignty of God over all the powers of history: "all flesh is grass . . . but the word of our God stands forever." A new theology of history arose, which could deal with the ambiguities of history and yet speak victoriously of Israel's calling. We may call this new tradition proto-apocalyptic, to distinguish it from classical prophecy which died with kingship, and from the full-blown apocalyptic tradition of the Hellenistic age.

The new view of Israel's history recognized an old age and a new age, the old things and the new, the old creation and the new. The old was passing away, the new dawning. There would be a new Exodus and a new conquest, a way for the redeemed to return to Zion.

Israel's vocation was now revealed more clearly. Israel's calling was that of the prophet, despised and rejected, upon whom the sins of the world were laid as upon an animal of sacrifice. By Israel's wounds, the nations were to be healed. But the time of Israel's exaltation is near. The law shall go forth to the nations. "Arise, shine, for your light has come, and the glory of the Lord has risen upon you. For behold darkness shall cover the earth and thick darkness the peoples; but the Lord will arise upon you and his glory will be seen upon you. And nations shall come to your light, and kings to the brightness of your rising." (Isaiah 60:1-3) The Lord will rule the earth from Zion.

We must look briefly in the Greek Bible for its

understanding of the vocation of Israel. Paul asks, "Has God cast off his people? Certainly not. . . . God has not cast off his people whom he foreknew." (Romans 11:1, 2) "I must repeat my question: Did [Israel] stumble so as to fall altogether? Certainly not. What has happened is this. By their stumble, salvation has come to the Gentiles . . ." (Romans 11:11) The New Testament, whether in the Gospels or in Paul, reflects the traditional doctrine of election.[1] The vocation of Israel is the salvation of the nations. "Salvation is of the Jews." There is a new dialectic in the Pauline teaching. God takes the occasion of Jewish disbelief in the Messiah to save the Gentiles, and in turn will use the Gentile church to provoke the jealousy of Israel. Among other things, the calling of the church in a mysterious way known to God will bring the full redemption of God's ancient people. "The secret is that a partial hardening has fallen on Israel, and will remain until the full number of the Gentiles has come in; when this is done, all Israel will be saved . . . for God does not go back on his acts of grace and calling" (Romans 11:25-29). In a striking metaphor, Paul speaks of the church as a "wild olive branch" grafted into the rich root of a domestic olive tree. The church thus affirms the biblical doctrine of election and recognizes Israel's covenant as eternal. It is the same covenant as that into which the Christian is grafted. The New Covenant is merely the ancient covenant, renewed in the new age. This is the Christian doctrine, its language taken from the prophets and Jewish apocalyptists.

2. The remarks above on the biblical doctrine of the vocation of Israel have evident pertinence

for Jewish-Christian relationships and for Jewish-Christian dialogue. The Christian affirms the validity and eternity of Israel's vocation. He recognizes that vocation as directed toward himself among the nations. He can never refer to Judaism as "another religion," or as a false form of the biblical faith. The church's calling requires that he enter into dialogue with the Jew, and his own salvation awaits the full redemption of Israel. His claim to be a new Israel is always made ambiguous by the existence of Israel "after the flesh."

Here rises a first obstacle to dialogue. The Jewish colleague might prefer a less tight embrace. The Jew has no obligation to recognize the vocation of the church, or to acknowledge the Christian's description of his vocation as suffering servant or prophet to the peoples. Contrary to Paul's prediction, he feels no jealousy of the church; he has learned to fear Christendom if not to despise it.

This brings us to the most formidable barrier to Jewish-Christian discourse: Auschwitz. Is not Auschwitz a final evidence of the moribundity of Western Christendom? Germany, a Christian state with an established church, attempted to destroy Jewry. It is not enough to say that the Western nations of largely Christian tradition wiped out Hitler and his works and established the State of Israel. It must be confessed that though Hitler's religion was Teutonic paganism, the weaknesses in Christianity contributed directly to the holocaust. One factor was Christian antinomianism, a heresy as old and as persistent in Christianity as Gnosticism, of which it is the child. Surely after Auschwitz the Christian is struck dumb, the Jew deaf. And yet the dialogue persists.

If the holocaust is the most profound practical
barrier to Jewish-Christian dialogue, perhaps the
most formidable theoretical barrier is to be found
in mythic or ahistorical views of revelation, which
have appeared from time to time in both Christianity and Judaism. By mythic I mean doctrines
that assert that revelation is direct, unconditioned
by the historical context in which it appears, un-
distorted by its reception by finite vehicles, un-
sullied by the human words in which it is cast. By
and large the biblical tradition assumes revelation
to be historical, mediate. The interpretations of
faith of a given age are not frozen into a final
form of divine truth, esoteric lore descended
from heaven, eternally valid. Such truth belongs
to mythic forms of discourse. On the contrary the
tradition of one biblical age is transformed by its
successor with perfect freedom. For example, each
successive tradent in the Pentateuch freely recasts
the traditional stuff received, reinterprets Israel's
history in new language, reframes ancient law in
forms relevant for its own age. The prophet in
particular reformulates ancient law that has become uncouth or irrelevant. He rarely cites ancient
tradition verbatim. He is primarily bent on interpreting God's new deeds and decisions in his
own time. Jewish apocalyptic casts itself into
more mythological forms of revelation, speeches
from heaven. And in apocalyptic, ancient myth
surges more freely than in earlier biblical tradition.
Yet here too we discern its essentially historical
mode of revelation, in the wild poetry of its
language, in its fecund multiplication of images,
events, visions, impressionistic, impatient with
consistency, unsystematic. It paints the picture of
the future with splashes of color, imprecise and

overlapping images, not with photographic precision or fidelity to rules of perspective.

We need not dwell on the high-handed way in which Jesus dealt with traditional law; and we need only allude to the freedom of the evangelists and of Paul in transforming and reinterpreting the traditions of Jesus and the primitive community. Paul, indeed, only in the rarest instances ever refers to words of Jesus.

Mythic doctrines of revelation belong to later ages in both Christianity and Judaism. Where they exist there can be no genuine dialogue. We can speak only of two religions, two systems of doctrine, each claiming absolute divine authority, each denying the other. In this context there can only be monologue, only the attempt to convert. If one asserts that the body of doctrine developed in Christian orthodoxy, or the body of tradition evolved in the Orthodox Judaism, bears the stamp of eternal validity, authorized by God and infallible, a claim made by both communities in later ages, he dare not enter into dialogue. Rabbi Soloveitchik has made this case cleanly and elegantly in his well-known article on Christian dialogue.[2] The act of entering into dialogue already compromises the faith.

It seems to me, however, that there are grounds for Jewish-Christian dialogue, solid grounds, well rooted in the doctrine of the vocation of Israel. Biblical revelation is historical, and Israel's vocation is a historical vocation. God has condescended to speak in particular historical contexts, and has not despised the inadequate symbols of human speech. Our faith is grounded in history, historically conditioned, exposed to the historian. There is a special precariousness and openness of such a historical religion. It is this peculiarity of the biblical tradition that provides a path to common discourse. At one level, the biblical tradition is exposed to critical and historical investigation. In principle if not in practice, the scholars of each community may reach consensus on the historical meaning of a scriptural tradition. Not only is the Hebrew Bible the common document of our faith; we are also committed to its historical interpretation. Ultimately we derive our doctrine and praxis from the Bible, and thus inevitably there is an openness to new interpretation and in turn to new forms in which we express our faith. Seen in one light the historical character of biblical revelation gives rise to a recognition of the precariousness of all our affirmations and institutions. Sinful and finite men, that is to say, historical creatures, know well that their most confident affirmations of faith are qualified if not distorted by the special historical context in which they are uttered.

Recent historical discovery and research has removed many obstacles to Jewish-Christian understanding. In the last century, the relationship between Judaism and Christianity was given classical formulation in terms of an idealistic dialectic which in turn was inspired by hyper-Lutheran definitions of freedom and law. Hegel's hatred of the law was perfect. He conceived biblical history as the story of the victory of freedom over law. Moses must play the role of villainous law giver, Jesus the role of heroic liberator. "[Moses] liberator of his nation," wrote Hegel, "was also its lawgiver; this could mean only that the man who had freed it from one yoke had laid

on it another," and by implication a more terrible
yoke. The reconstruction of biblical religion in
later formulations viewed Christianity as the child
of biblical prophecy, the free and ethical impulse
in Israelite religion, Judaism as child of the the-
ocratic and legal impulse of the post exilic Jewish
community. Historical study, Christian and Jewish, has put to flight these formulations and con-
structions once for all. To put it simply, perhaps
overly simply, we now see clearly that both Judaism and Christianity were in no small part the
children of apocalypticism.[3] This new construction on the relationship between the separate
communities stemmed from studies of Jewish
apocalyptic, and from studies in the origins of
Jewish mysticism. The recovery of the Essene
library of Qumrân has provided an astounding
confirmation of these trends in historical study.
Late pre-Christian Judaism now looks very different from the syntheses of a past generation, of
which the works of George Foote Moore are
typical. It was infinitely richer and more diverse
than we had guessed. The apocalypticism of
Qumrân looked so strange to one distinguished
professor of the Hebrew University that he attempted to prove that the library stemmed from
Christian antinomians of the second century of
the common era. One may contrast the reactions
of a Christian scholar who argued that the documents of Qumrân are typically Pharisaic, without
bearing upon our understanding of Christian origins. Neither Jew nor Christian is particularly
enchanted by the notion that Christianity is fully
continuous with impulses in pre-Christian Judaism.

I must confess that as a historian of biblical religion and the origins of Christianity and Judaism, I am pressed to the view that rabbinic Judaism and Christianity are complementary traditions, each developing directly from major impulses in the Judaism of the pre-Christian era. To say that Judaism and Christianity are complementary does not mean merely that both are legitimate developments of the biblical community. Neither Jew nor Christian is interested in receiving the stamp of legitimacy from the other. I think though that it can be argued that each preserved certain valid insights or doctrines of the biblical community lost in the other, and that both Christianity and Judaism have in subsequent development distorted the primitive faith as well as evolved beyond it, and vis-à-vis each other have tended to polarize. I am tempted to say that both communities are heretical strains or caricatures of biblical Israel. I am able to say, at least, that this appears to me to be a fair description of my own tradition. Certainly Christianity is not whole apart from Judaism.

This brings us again to the dialectic of Paul: that the calling of each community is to lure the other to faithfulness and obedience. Let us take one example to illustrate my meaning.

To the Christian, I believe, Auschwitz is properly a symbol of the moribundity of the Christian doctrine of law. There is insufficient time to trace the complex history of the Christian understanding of the role of grace and law in the community of the faithful. The tendency to deny any redeeming feature gracing law is as old as Gnosticism, and Christian antinomianism was not overthrown

in the debates of the Reformation. Already Paul,
adopting a radically apocalyptic understanding of
law, bypassed Moses to seize on Abraham's covenant of grace. From the synagogue the Christian
can and must learn the role of law in the redeemed
community.

There are two points of confusion here. There
is the notion that the covenant of Sinai is a covenant of works, the covenant of Abraham a
covenant of grace. Neither the Hebrew Bible nor
the Jewish tradition in its normative formulations
permits such confusion. The two covenants are
one covenant just as the eternal covenant of Israel
is identical with the new or rather the renewed
covenant of the new age. And neither is a covenant of works. The only context of law in the
Bible is the context of grace. The Decalogue be-
gins: "I am the Lord who has called you and
redeemed you, therefore . . . thou shalt."

A second point of confusion arises in the Christian understanding of the age of redemption.
There is a gnostic tendency to regard the age of
redemption as present. We forget that we live
after Mt. Sinai, before Armageddon, after the
coming of Jesus, before the glorification of Christ.
We too easily forget that we who are called into
faith and freed from our bonds persist in our sin.
Our minds are stupid, our ears fat. We are des-
perate for a guide, for the illumination of the law.
In our circumstances, "the law of the Lord is
perfect, restoring the soul, the testimony of the
Lord is sure, making wise the simple, the precepts
of the Lord are right, rejoicing the heart." (Psalm
19:7-8) The Christian supposing the law a curse
to Israel needs to look to the dancing of the fes-

tival of *simhat Torah* and recover the doctrine of law as guide to the redeemed, its *usus renatus*.

I wonder if in the teaching of Paul we do not find the basis for a doctrine of the complementarity of the two faiths. So far as our age is concerned, this would give validity to a doctrine of historical pluralism. In God's plan the two biblical communities are to remain separate, side by side, each with its integrity and special calling until the end. The restoration of oneness to the synagogue and church belongs only to the kingdom of God, and it may be that even in that age of reconciliation the unity of the community of God will include rich diversity of which the diversities of Judaism and Christianity are as broken images.

[1] See also Amos Wilder's excellent study, "The Church and Israel in the Light of Election," *Studia Evangelica,* IV, ed. F. L. Cross (Berlin, 1968), pp. 347-357; and *Antijudaismus im Neuen Testament,* ed. W. P. Eckert, et al. (Munich, 1967).
[2] "Confrontation," *Tradition* 6:2 (1964), pp. 5-29. Cf. K. Stendahl, "Judaism and Christianity II," *Harvard Divinity Bulletin* (Autumn 1967), pp. 2-9; reprinted in *Cross Currents* 17 (1967), pp. 445-458.
[3] Cf. F. M. Cross, "New Directions in the Study of Apocalyptic," *Journal for Theology and the Church* (1969).

THEOLOGICAL
ANTI-SEMITISM IN
THE NEW TESTAMENT

Rosemary Ruether

Fundamental to Christian self-understanding is discussion of basic structures of Christian thought which imply that Christianity is God's new dispensation to man, and which do so in such a manner as to imply that Judaism is an obsolete religion, a surpassed form of God's relation to man. In undertaking a consideration of Christianity and Judaism in these terms I am of course aware that such structures of thought are not just incidental, and that in questioning them we are posing a radical question to Christianity about the validity of its own gospel.

That the concern in recent years for Jewish-Christian dialogue has arisen more from the Christian than from the Jewish side doubtless arises from a tardily awakened Christian sense of guilt and responsibility for the historical treatment of Jews in Christian lands, a history culminating in the death camps. Becoming more sensitive to how traditional presentations of Christianity have been molded in an anti-Semitic form, Christians have begun to acknowledge that Christianity itself is culpably involved in the evil history of anti-Semitism. So far, however, the question has not been raised among Christians in a really radical manner. Christians have been willing to acknowledge an element of anti-Semitism as accidental to Christianity, but not as something deeply rooted in the gospel itself. They have been willing to acknowledge the existence of anti-Semitic preaching, even in the heart of Christian worship, but only as a sign of misunderstanding, as distortion of true Christianity.

All this means that the discussion of anti-Semitism has been confined to sociological relations between Christians and Jews. Anti-Semitism has been explained in this context, with every effort made to keep the discussion off the territory of the gospel itself. Insofar as negative attitudes toward Jews are recognized in the New Testament, they too are attributed to sociological relations between Christians and Jews in the New Testament period. Moreover, even in this admission there tend to linger overtones of the suggestion that Judaism in the first century was in some kind of bad moral or spiritual state which, accepted as historical fact, both caused and justifies the New Testament description of the "blindness" of the Jews and their "rejection" of the gospel.

This careful hedging on New Testament territory was particularly apparent in the Vatican Council II decree on the Jews. In theological terms, it was willing to go only so far as to repudiate the idea of a special guilt vis-à-vis the death of Jesus resting on the Jewish people for all time. Since Christianity takes the death of Jesus as a sacrifice for sin on behalf of all mankind, it was easy enough to shift the discussion onto this framework, to assert that the Jewish guilt in this regard was only an instance of the general guilt of all mankind, not one pertaining to Jews alone. But this statement was framed in such a way as to prevent the raising of any questions about anti-Semitic attitudes within the New Testament itself. Whatever attitudes toward the Jews might be found in the New Testament were unimpeachable, both theologically and historically. This was territory which could not be challenged!

I propose to challenge this territory, and to do so on theological rather than on historical grounds. That is to say, I do not set out merely to question certain factual aspects of the New Testament account, such as the possibility that later antagonisms between Christians and Jews may have caused schematized, negative presentations of the Jews, especially the Pharisees. Nor will I deal with the even more crucial question of the truth of the New Testament account of the crucifixion; there have already been thorough studies in this area. Various Jewish scholars in particular have pointed to the untenability of the New Testament account of the crucifixion in the light of first century Jewish religious and political life. Further, it is now fairly well established that the New Testament account is an apologetic reworking of history to shift the blame from the Roman to the Jewish authorities. I prefer to consider basic theological structures in New Testament thought which imply an anti-Semitic stance within the gospel itself, not simply in the historical or sociological accidents that may have surrounded its inception. In other words, I propose to discuss those fundamental kinds of judgments which cannot be corrected without total rethinking of the Christian message itself.

In order to approach this level of theological anti-Semitism I will focus on three basic concepts: (1) The idea of Jesus as the Christ; i.e., the assumption that since the Messiah has already come as a historical event, the Jews have rejected the savior promised by God as the fulfillment of their own religious destiny. (2) The idea of the New Testament; i.e., the implication that God has made a new covenant with a new people and has passed over or left behind the Jews, who now become the people of the "Old Testament," the old covenant; whenever Christians refer to the Jewish Bible as the "Old Testament" they take for granted this judgment upon Judaism. (3) The idea of law and grace, or law and gospel, as it is found in St. Paul and accepted in all Christian theology—though with particular vigor by Protestantism—as the fundamental way to describe the situation of man through the work of Christ in contrast with that old, superseded situation of man represented by the life of Judaism under the Law. These three ideas, axiomatic in Christian theology, add up to a judgment on Judaism which can hardly be underestimated.

One could hardly say anything worse about Judaism than that it has rejected the Messiah; to say this is to hold that Judaism has abandoned its own covenant and promise. Built into the treatment of the Jewish and Christian Bibles as Old and New Testaments respectively is the idea of Judaism as a superseded and obsolete religion, superseded not simply historically but theologically, superseded in terms of the covenant of God with Israel itself.

In this respect it does no good to stress the church's "continuity" with Israel, as is often done.

For such continuity is allowed only in the form of inheritance of the truths of the Old Covenant in light of the higher truth of the New Covenant which has taken up and absorbed the old truths into itself, thereby rendering the continued independent existence of the religion of the "Old Testament" superfluous. It is perhaps not accidental that Christian knowledge of Judaism normally stops short at the first century, and that Talmud and Midrash, as well as the rest of Jewish history, are usually unknown to Christian students. Certainly the cutoff seems to imply an unspoken judgment to the effect that the continued existence of Judaism, while historically a fact, is somehow illegitimate, and that to study it is to concede to it an existence to which it has no right.

Finally, the dichotomy of law and grace comes very close to equating the very heart of Jewish religion with sin—a tendency particularly strong in the Protestant traditions which lean on the Pauline dichotomy. Man's dilemma is here seen as apostasy from God, represented by man's desire to save himself autonomously; self-salvation, as the heart of man's entrapment; the religion of the Law, as the prime example of such self-salvation. Thus the Law becomes the central symbol of sin and the fall of man.

The fundamental nature of this axiom can also be seen in Protestant treatment of Roman Catholicism—an interpretation true not only of Reformation polemics but of modern Protestant theology as well. In Barth, for example, Judaism, Roman Catholicism and Protestant liberalism are lumped together (in descending order of intrinsicality) as instances of this same epidemic. Indeed, in many ways Protestantism has patterned its view of its relation to Roman Catholicism on a model provided by the relationship of the gospel to the religion of the Law. The possibility of including the "fallen" church in this model does not, however, soften the judgment upon Judaism, but reveals how axiomatic it is. Judaism is again seen as the prime instance of what Christian theology takes to be both false religion and the theological situation of the "old man," with the "fallen" church recapitulating this fall and sliding back into a condition of presalvational infidelity.

These remarks should be sufficient to suggest how serious are the anti-Semitic implications of these axiomatic structures of Christian thought. Our next task is to examine the roots of these theological symbols in the New Testament, and ask whether their interpretation in Christian theology, and indeed in the New Testament itself, is legitimate. We must begin by realizing that all these Christian symbols (Messiah, New Covenant, the era of grace which surpasses the Law) have their roots in prophetic Judaism. Indeed, since they are drawn from ideas basic to Jewish faith they imply a truly devastating judgment upon Judaism. Nonetheless, they are interpreted in Christianity in ways which Judaism must reject as spurious and illegitimate.

This is the heart of the chasm between Christianity and Judaism. It is such a fundamental chasm that it would seem to preclude any Jewish-Christian theological ecumenism. Each side must affirm its own theological identity in such a way as to invalidate the existence of the other. Although the two groups might agree to get along with each

other as purely human societies, may even share
common humanistic endeavors, theologically they
would seem to be irrevocably divided.

However, since all these Christian concepts
have their roots in prophetic Judaism (which current Judaism accepts while rejecting the Christian
interpretation of the terms), it would seem that
this is the best place to begin the discussion, if
there can be any discussion at all. Here, of course,
I am caught in a dilemma—pretending to carry on
both sides of the dialogue, which is not possible. I
cannot really speak for the Jewish side, but I can
try to show why I think the Jewish rejection of
the Christian interpretation is substantially justified, and why, if Christians are to understand the
meaning of the symbols, they must "interpret
them back" into their original prophetic context.
This implies of course that the Christian way of
interpreting the terms is in fact a misinterpreta-
tion, and that the Christian church which takes its
stand on that interpretation rests on dubious
grounds theologically, however much it may seem
to have won the right to its interpretation through
historical success.

The root of the disagreement lies in interpretation of the terms. Judaism understands them as
eschatological symbols appropriate only to the full
and complete advent of the kingdom of God;
Christianity, as historical events applicable to the
founding of a new historical religion.

To arrive at an understanding of this distinction, let us start with the idea of the Christ.
"Christ" originally meant "Messiah," although in
Christian theology it has taken on meanings quite
foreign to the original Jewish idea. Since Chris-

tians identify "Christ" with the historical Jesus of
Nazareth, they are prone to exaggerate the expectation of a messianic person in biblical religion.
Actually the Bible puts less stress on a Messianic
person than on the expectation of a Messianic *age*
—the age of the fulfillment of the promise, when
God's will shall be done on earth, when man will
live in perfect harmony with God, with his fellow
man and with all creation. That age is not necessarily thought of as an immortal one. Originally it
was looked on as a temporal period, for man himself is intrinsically temporal. It was projected as a
future historical period, but one in which all
things would be as they should be.

Only occasionally does the symbol of the Messiah as the deputy of God in bringing in this new
age and as the ruler of the kingdom appear in
messianic prophecy. He is not so much the central
idea as simply a part of the apparatus of the symbolism of the kingdom. This kingdom is never
understood simply as an inward kingdom. Inward
obedience is indeed an intrinsic part of it, but it is
seen in inseparable relation to the flowering of all
nature and human society into the perfect goodness desired by God. Hence in prophetic terms it
is quite meaningless to speak of the Messiah as
having come when the kingdom has not come.
Certainly a casual glance around the world and at
the course of human history to date is sufficient to
make it obvious that the coming has not taken
place.

One Christian answer to this concept has been
that the Jews had some gross, materialistic concept of the kingdom which was rightfully disappointed, and that the true inner kingdom of the

Spirit has indeed come and dwells in our hearts. But this reply is really without foundation. There is only one biblical idea of the kingdom—the kingdom in which the lion lies down with the lamb and men beat their swords into plowshares. Hence from a Jewish perspective it is simply meaningless to speak of Christ as an event that has already taken place, much less one that took place almost 2,000 years ago—before all the wars, misery and injustice that have multiplied from that time until now.

In similar fashion, the ideas of the New Covenant and the inward obedience from the heart that surpasses the obedience of the Law had meaning in prophetic Judaism as eschatological visions, not as realities which could become past historical events within the world as it is. As it appears in Christian Scriptures, the passage in Jeremiah 31:31-34 is fundamental to this idea of the New Covenant and grace. When Christianity saw itself as the people of the New Covenant, the people who have been given a new power to obey from the heart, they were understanding themselves as the eschatological community fulfilling the prophetic description foretold by Jeremiah:

Behold, the days are coming, says the Lord, when I will make a new covenant with the house of Israel and the house of Judah, not like the covenant which I made with their fathers when I took them by the hand to bring them out of the land of Egypt, my covenant which they broke, though I was their husband, says the Lord. But this is the covenant which I will make with the house of Israel after those days, says the Lord: I will put my law within them, and I will write it upon their hearts; and I will be their God, and they shall be my people. No longer shall each man teach his neighbor and each his brother, saying, "Know the Lord," for they shall all know me, from the least of them to the greatest, says the Lord; for I will forgive their iniquity and remember their sin no more.

The whole Christian idea of the New Covenant, the New Testament, the era of forgiveness and grace which surpasses the external teaching of the Law, when every man is given a new heart—all this springs from the prophetic description of the messianic era appearing here.

Paul's doctrine of law and grace is based on his own interpretation of this passage, sifted through his conversion experience but grounded on his Jewish expectation of an age when God would forgive men's sins and give him a new heart, when external teaching would pass away and each man would obey from within. But because Paul knew very well that this fulfillment lay in the messianic age, his doctrine of grace—indeed the whole of early Christian use of the symbols of Christ, New Covenant, the outpouring of the Holy Spirit, the resurrection and so on—depended on his listeners' faith as apocalyptic Jews that the decisive turn of the ages was actually beginning in the events surrounding the life and death of Jesus as proclaimed in the Christian community, and that this cosmic revolution, begun in the death and resurrection of Jesus, would shortly be consummated in the return of Jesus as victorious Son of Man.

In other words, all these symbols originally operated within Christianity only as an expression of an ecstatic understanding of the birth of the church as literally the beginning of the kingdom. Early Christianity was born in an ecstatic moment of apocalyptic expectation, and the primitive church appropriated its symbols in the context of the faith of Jews who saw themselves as standing in the cataclysmic moment of world transformation. They themselves stood at the crisis point at which the old evil was passing away and the kingdom of God was dawning.

To speak of their leader as the Christ (or rather as he who would shortly return as the Christ, for he had been the Christ only in a hidden form in his lifetime); to speak of the outpouring of the Spirit (as in Acts 2:16-20) as the apocalyptic Day of the Lord; to speak to Christians as the people of the New Covenant; to speak of grace and spiritual worship surpassing the outward obedience of the Law—all this was meaningful in a Jewish context, expressions by people who believed that the fulfillment of the expectations of their Jewish faith was in fact coming to pass. They were thus convinced only because they believed quite literally that the cosmic revolution was happening here and now, that Jesus was the first fruits of those who are to rise from the dead, that very soon this lingering form of the old era would vanish, and that they who believed in him would be catapulted into the kingdom of God to meet their glorious leader who would descend on clouds of glory.

We have here no possibility of a new historical era, some new religious institution, some new historical dispensation. Originally none of the symbols was understood as expressing the foundation of a new religion. Rather, the symbols were affirmed in full continuity with their original prophetic meaning; it was literally believed that world history was at an end and the kingdom of God at hand.

What happened when the timetable for the return of Jesus as the Christ was exceeded beyond all credibility, when the generation which was to be the last generation of history began to die out, to be supplanted by their children and their children's children, when the cosmic crisis came to no decisive head but just dribbled along in the same old tiresome fashion? From a Jewish perspective, the honest thing would have been to say, "Well, I guess we were wrong about the Christ coming and the new age beginning." But of course the Christians didn't, perhaps couldn't, do that. They had too much vested emotional interest in the things which they had felt and experienced, which surely must have meant something, which surely couldn't just have been a mistake.

So the work of reinterpretation gradually set in, to be carried out in two basic ways. One was the spiritualizing of the eschatological, the other the historicizing of the eschatological.

To spiritualize the eschatological early Christianity drew on gnostic and Hellenistic philosophical ideas which understood eternity as essentially above man, cohering with his inward spiritual nature. In this sense the eschatological is interpreted as the transcendent; thus it could be seen as coming to man within his higher spiritual nature, even though the outward course of history proceeded much as before. We find this spiritualizing of the eschatological particularly in the Gospel of John.

The historicizing of the eschatological, found particularly in the Gospel of Luke, corresponds to what New Testament scholars call "early Catholicism." The gospel of the coming of Christ was interpreted in terms of a new timetable of salvation history. The final eschatological culmination of world history in the kingdom was detached from the ideas of Christ, the resurrection, the outpouring of the Spirit and the New Covenant and pushed off into an indefinite by-and-by. Meanwhile these events, originally understood as the ecstatic signs of the approaching kingdom, were interpreted as historical events—the founding of a new religion, a new religious organization, a new world era.

It was precisely this historicizing of the eschatological symbols that was responsible for their interpretation in anti-Semitic fashion. Earlier interpreted ecstatically as the beginning of the kingdom, they sprang from the heart of prophetic faith and were understood as the fulfillment of that faith. Interpreted now historically, for a church which had become largely Gentile, they were understood as events that had already taken place, establishing in history a new era and a new people which superseded and rendered obsolete the historical existence of the religion from which they had come. Thus under the threat of continued history the church, which originally had projected no historical existence for herself but had seen herself as the Israel of the kingdom, won a historical existence for herself by negating and claiming to supersede the historical existence of Israel.

This historicization seems to me fundamentally invalid in terms of the original meaning of the symbols. The dawning new age can be experienced ecstatically as a power which comes to us from the future and momentarily catches us up in its embrace. But once that ecstasy fades the experience of newness cannot be carried over into a new historical institution, cannot be made the foundation of its self-proclamation, particularly not the means of discarding some other people. Once the idea of the new covenant ceases to stand within the context of a people who can identify with the original covenant, when it stands as the historical foundation of another group, it fundamentally betrays the original prophetic meaning.

The prophet could speak of "that covenant which you broke, even though I brought you out of Egypt" only because he identified with that community which was brought out of the land of Egypt. Once such a prophecy is used outside the context of that community to discard and supersede it, the prophecy is used invalidly and even blasphemously. Such, for example, is the use of Old Testament prophecies of wrath in Christian Good Friday services as a polemic "against the Jews."

Thus in order for Christianity to stand validly within the biblical religion it must first of all recognize thoroughly that all its theological symbols must be returned to their original prophetic context. This means that the concepts of resurrection, the outpouring of the Spirit, the people of the New Covenant and the new age, finally even the Christ, cannot be appropriated as historical events which lie behind us as institutional foundations. Rather, they must remain eschatological, must loom ahead of us as realities toward which we are still moving.

Christianity does not supersede Judaism in

terms of the covenant of God with man in history;
at the very most it is an extending of that covenant to peoples not previously included in its symbols. But the covenant under which it moves in
history is still the one covenant of Abraham and
Moses, the covenant which we continually break
even though God leads us out of Egypt by the
hand. So theologically Christianity cannot see itself as ahead of or superseding Judaism, as already
encamping in (much less usurping) the promised
land. *Coram deo* Christianity is still in the same
historical situation as Judaism, indeed as is mankind as a whole: making its way through the
desert, accompanied by many a golden idol and
broken tablet, between Exodus and the promised
land.

Once all false historicization of the eschatological is abandoned it is possible that the Christian
experience may be found as a contribution to the
understanding of the biblical tradition in a way
which no longer sets up a chasm between the
peoples of the biblical faith. It seems to me that
the problem with the traditional Jewish understanding of the kingdom is that the kingdom remained solely future, and was interpreted in such
a literally historical framework that it could never
in any sense become present without implying the
advent of conditions which never obtain within
historical existence. The kingdom was understood
as a future historical period and at the same time
as a period which can never come in history.

Hence Judaism was bound to an essentially
tragic expectation of the kingdom as the longed-
for era, ever expected but never here. Again and
again it seemed to draw near, filling Jews with

the power of its coming. But once that experience
passed and history continued along much the
same lines as before, the experience could be interpreted only as a false experience, a false Messiah, to be totally repudiated. Judaism was thus
returned to a hope which never came and could
only create madness, despair, cynicism or loss of
faith in God.

The events surrounding the birth of Christianity
constituted one such moment, perhaps the greatest. For Jews, expectation seemed close to fulfillment; they tasted the sweetness of the approaching kingdom, only to have history cheat them of
its fruits. Judaism could then only repudiate what
had happened as another instance of the appearance of a false Messiah. Meanwhile those who
failed to be recalled to the old situation of expectation had to objectify their own experience and
thus create a schismatic, polemical view of their
relationship to Judaism.

Is there another alternative? Is there a way of
understanding the eschatological as a reality that,
while remaining essentially future, can draw near
and become proleptically present, without abso-
lutizing that presence and turning it into an objective datum? Is it possible to speak of "Christ
events" within history while acknowledging that
the foundation of those events does not lie behind
us in some objective historical event of the coming
of Christ but remains essentially future?

Judaism has not been able to entertain such a
dehistoricized view of the kingdom; for it, the
kingdom either comes or it doesn't. There are no
"kingdom presences" which stir us up—give us
new power for some moment of historical creativ-

ity, only to be relativized by the ongoing march of history. But this also means that Judaism has been stuck with a tragic experience of the kingdom as the always unfulfilled hope. Christianity, on the other hand, has believed that the kingdom could become present, at least as an initial down payment. But it has historicized this as a coming of Christ, an event that took place once and for all in history (now become an untenably distant past history).

Is it possible that a meeting ground might be found between these two views, whereon we could acknowledge that by its very nature the Christ event, the coming of the kingdom, can never become a past historical "fact," but rather that it remains essentially future, transcendent, eschatological?

This transcendent future, without losing its essential futurity, can draw near and become proleptically present. In such moments we are stirred to an ecstatic vision of an absolute future, are given power to make a great leap of historical creativity. Every such moment partakes of the decisive *kairos* of the coming of the kingdom. Nevertheless such moments, while partaking of the absolute and decisive moment, fade back into history once their power is spent. There they become relative moments, which may bear good fruit or bad. We do not need to objectify and absolutize these moments, because the eschatological, while made present, is not simply immanentized in them but remains still and always ahead of us, drawing us on from whatever accomplishments we may have achieved under its inspira-

tion in the past, always available for a new insight
in the future which may stand in judgment upon
the previous accomplishment.

Such an understanding of the eschatological as
the principle of self-transcendence in history, as a
power which can become proleptically present and
fruitful of creative work but is never wholly immanentized in such work, that remains essentially
ahead of us, always available for new self-
transcendence—such a view may be a key for solv-
ing the theological dilemma that stands between
Christianity and Judaism. If the key is to work,
Christianity will have to recognize its own experience of Jesus not as the absolute coming of Christ
but rather as a relative instance of the drawing
near of the eschatological. Indeed, is not this view
already suggested in the Christian doctrine that
we still look forward to the "final" coming?

By the same token, Christians might then be
able to recognize other events as the presently
more decisive experience of the coming of Christ
for others. For American Negroes, perhaps Malcolm X might stand as such a symbol; for Jews,
the recent taking of Jerusalem.

Once Christians, Jews and others who share
biblical modes of thinking can see the Christ as a
power that can become proleptically present without losing its essentially transcendent character,
they can perhaps begin to recognize the moments
which were decisive for them in a contextual way.
They can cease to impose and threaten each other
with their own moments of truth, to seek to invalidate each other in some cosmic court. We can
each rejoice in the moment of truth as it comes

to us and then let it go when its hour is done, knowing that we remain essentially wayfaring people traveling through the desert; that the promised land, tasted briefly at this or that oasis, is never completed in history but remains always ahead of us.

JUDAISM AND CHRISTIANITY: THEN AND NOW

Krister Stendahl

In his recent book, *The Meaning and End of Religion,* Wilfred Cantwell Smith of McGill and, presently, of Harvard, has drawn to a pointed conclusion the uneasiness which scholars have felt for some time when using the word "religion," not to say "religions." His warnings are much to the point when we try to speak about Judaism and Christianity.

"Christianity" and "Judaism" are abstractions. The given is not a religion but a people, a church, a community with its history, its traditions, its claims, its witness, its attempts to relate itself to an ever-changing world. If we were to use a not too attractive image we could say that the abstraction "Christianity" is just the skin which the snake sheds every so often. It can be handled and studied in many ways. But the living reality is the church, the people with its organic continuity and complexity through the ages. And the same applies of course to Judaism. To speak about Christianity and Judaism as two religions already forecloses many of the possibilities to understand what happened, happens, and might happen.

At the present time the popular image of the

relationship between Judaism and Christianity is well expressed in two distinct habits of speech. On the one hand there is the reference to The Three Faiths of America: Catholics, Protestants, and Jews. On the other hand there is the more academic construct The Hebrew-Christian Tradition. Both of these "models" exert a powerful influence on our culture and our thinking. While theology is to many a highly technical and suspect term, it is no secret that such expressions harbor whole theologies, partly conscious but mainly unconscious. It is reasonable to ask whether these theologies are well founded, sound and honest.

To speak about The Three Faiths is perhaps dubious already since it suggests that a Hindu, a Buddhist, a Muslim, an agnostic or an atheist could not be a true American. But it is not necessary to draw that arrogant conclusion. More serious is the implicit suggestion that the relation and the distance between these three faiths is somehow of the same order. This is further complicated by the fact that, due to the given majority/minority ratio in a community, we often get a constellation of Protestants and Jews versus Catholics. Yet, from many points of view, Catholics and Protestants would be expected to have a great deal more in common than such a pattern suggests. And also Judaism has *its* catholics and protestants. It becomes increasingly clear that the pattern of The Three Faiths is a construct in which the nontheological factors easily gain the upper hand. That does not diminish its significance. But it makes us anxious not to extend this significance beyond its own limitations.

The expression, The Hebrew-Christian Tradition, is more at home in colleges and universities, in the survey courses of the humanities. It sees this tradition as having furnished the Western world with certain indispensable ideas and ideals, often epitomized as justice and compassion. It presupposes that the significant elements in Judaism and Christianity are those which they have in common, not those which divide them. If The Three Faiths are nontheological in the direction toward the sociological, The Hebrew-Christian Tradition is nontheological in the direction toward the philosophical and ethical. It should also be noted that the Christian imperialism exerts its pressure on how this tradition is usually handled in higher education. The component "Hebrew" often stands for what Christians call the Old Testament, and once Christianity is on the scene this "Hebrew" element is absorbed in the Christian tradition. Little or no attention is given to Jewish history and thought after 70 or 135 C.E. Maimonides may be a footnote to Thomas, the Jewishness a footnote to Spinoza, and Hasidism is not mentioned at all. Thereby the expression The Hebrew-Christian Tradition becomes more manageable, but the term pays little more than lip service to the actual relationship between Judaism and Christianity. It does not need to be that way, of course, and it may well be that the formula The Hebrew-Christian Tradition could function more adequately in our search for a viable understanding of the relations between Judaism and Christianity. Even so, we should not forget that it of necessity puts a premium on similarities rather than differences, thereby prejudging the case before us.

Whatever the respective and relative assets and

liabilities of these two models, habits of speech or even slogans, we cannot stress too emphatically that they are good and highly significant signs of a positive climate; a climate which the Western world has seldom known, and the Christian majority has seldom allowed. A climate in which we may be able to take a new look at the relationships. Without sounding more prophetic than we have the right to be, we could see the present situation in America as a unique and fresh challenge to our own generation of theological scholarship. The Jewish and the Christian communities find themselves side by side without many of the man-made walls which earlier separated them socially, culturally, intellectually. In both communities this proves to be a blessing, and it has driven us to a deeper grasp of our separate identities as believers. This is the time and the place and the climate in which we dare and we must question these models. We can and we must ask whether they are as well conceived as they were well intentioned and have proven pragmatically beneficial.

It is my contention that, in the long run, a onesided stress on the common elements, or a non-theological acceptance of a sociological status quo with its mutual and, hopefully, increased respect for one another, cannot be the final chapter. That climate constitutes rather the first pages of a new volume in the history of the debate out of which the Christian church was born. The time has come for resuming that debate, which was cut off prematurely and transformed into an unusually grim history of everything ugly from name calling to pogroms and holocaust.

I am not sure that the image is a happy one, but for whatever it is worth, we need a certain type of historical psychoanalysis, by which we are made aware of what happened in that most early infancy when the nascent church emerged out of its Jewish matrix and when the first steps were taken. Without serious attempts to recapture that most significant stage in the life of the Christian Church, new and free and fearless action may well be impossible.

It is well known to contemporaries that we know a good deal more about those early years than we did a hundred years ago. But such knowledge is slow in affecting the sentiments and the systematic thinking of the present. Contemporary biblical and Jewish studies may have many weak points, but they have developed a very impressive ability to distinguish the actual issues of the past from the ways in which these issues appeared to later generations, our own included.

Let us then turn to a few areas where I think a changed picture of the past might affect the questions of the present and rectify the future debate between Judaism and Christianity.

1. The understanding of Jesus depends heavily on how one reads what we Christians call the Old Testament. In a time when the red thread through that Old Testament was seen to be ethical monotheism and where the prophets were hailed and measured by that canon, Jesus became to the Christians the super-prophet. His greatness was asserted by demonstrating—often on shaky grounds —that his ethics was higher and his monotheism was purer and warmer than ever before in Israel or in the world at large.

We are now very much aware of how such a perspective on the Old Testament, while congenial to the 19th century in the West, is alien to the perspective of the Scriptures. We have learned to see the Old Testament centered in the people of the covenant, with its Torah, its cult, its psalms, its wisdom and proverbs, its prophets and their promises. We see an Old Testament which points toward an Age to Come, an Old Testament which leads to eschatology and messianism.

2. This new picture was mainly drawn on the basis of a better analysis of the Old Testament texts in their historical context, but it was highly confirmed and corroborated by the increased concern for and knowledge about the so-called Intertestamental Literature with its apocalyptic intensity and religious vitality. All this came to the attention of a wider public with the much celebrated find of the library of the Qumrân community, the Dead Sea Scrolls. Here was a Jewish community where the strict obedience to the Law was an integral part of its eschatology, even to the point of an anticipatory realization of the New Covenant. Their common meal was a foretaste of the Messianic banquet.

3. Different in structure and yet not unrelated to the sentiments of the age, Pharisaism can be understood in categories which had been utterly submerged in the anachronistic alternatives of legalism and grace. Pharisaism becomes a serious and honorable way of living in expectation and obedience, an obedience which is motivated and warmed by the expectation and an expectation in concrete and flexible obedience.

4. In such a setting all that is said and came to

be said of Jesus has its genetic center in the claim
that he was the Messiah, that with him or through
him the messianic age had drawn nigh. His teaching, his actions, his gracious and his harsh words
all relate to this one claim. It would be wrong to
say that he came to teach a better concept of love,
a deeper concept of repentance, a more spiritual
concept of the kingdom. All these concepts were
there, warm, deep and spiritual enough. But, to
him, so close was the kingdom, so closely did he
believe himself related to its coming, that he dared
to apply its glorious gifts and standards here and
now. And often—I think to his own surprise—the
publicans and the sinners were more willing to
listen and follow than were the professed religious.
Thereby both the grace and the judgment were
heightened immeasurably in the very structure of
the gospel.

5. There is increasing evidence that the role of
Pilate was considerably greater in the execution
of Jesus than the tradition and even the gospels
lead us to think. The precise role of the Jewish
leaders we cannot assess. The nature of the sources
makes it unlikely that we ever will. The crucifixion—a Roman execution—speaks its clear language, indicating that Jesus must have appeared
sufficiently messianic, not only in a purely spiritual
sense, to constitute a threat to political order according to Roman standards. At this very point we
can discern one of the earliest signs of how tensions between Judaism and Christianity have
affected the writing of history. Already in the
gospels two tendencies are at work. The role of
the Roman official, Pilate, is minimized—it was
not easy in the Empire to have a founder who had

been crucified by a Roman procurator; and the
"no" of the Jews was the theological basis on
which Paul and other missionaries claimed the
right to bring the gospel to the gentiles. "He came
to his own, but his own received him not . . ."—
". . . and the vineyard will be given to other
tenants who will deliver to him the produce when
the time comes." Under the pressure of these two
tendencies, one political and one theological, the
exact events of history have been lost, as to the
interplay between the members of the Sanhedrin
and Pontius Pilate. But it is reasonable to see the
latter as the key figure.

6. Thus the messianic issue in all its Jewishness
stands in the center of Christian origins. What else
could we expect when "Christian" actually is only
the Greek for "Messianic." I do not consider it an
overstatement to say that the whole Christological
development of Christianity, even to that famous
intensity of the fourth century should be seen as a
development from its original and Jewish nucleus:
Jesus Christ. That is the creed: I believe that Jesus
is the Messiah; and its chiastic correlate: the
Messiah is Jesus.

There is one point in the early stages of this
Christological development which needs special
attention. If we were to say, as we often do, that
the Christian believes that the Messiah has come,
while the Jew still lives in expectation, then we
use at least highly unprecise language.

In one of the earliest Christological expressions
found in the New Testament we hear Peter say:
Repent . . . that times of refreshment may come
from the Lord and he may send the Messiah who
was appointed for you, i.e. Jesus, whom heaven

must keep until the time of consummation . . .
(Acts 3:19-21). Here the coming of the Messiah
Jesus is still future. Peter here shares with the
Jewish community the faith in the Parousia, which
is the consummation, the Age to Come. He an-
nounces that their Messiah will be this Jesus.
While later Christians came to assert the "first
coming" of Jesus in his earthly ministry but had
highly divided opinion about the so called "second coming," the earliest Christians were clear
about the Coming, the Parousia, which they
looked forward to, together with their Jewish
brethren. *Their* problem was to find the right
answer to the question: In what sense and to what
extent was the life and death of Jesus a coming
of the Messiah? This is the problem to which the
different gospels, and the traditions underlying
them, give their answers, some tentative, some
increasingly clear.

In the earliest stages of this development the
claim that the messianic age had come and was
truly inaugurated, that its powers were at work in
the world through the church, centered around
the resurrection and the spirit. These were the
decisive signs that the new age was here. The
general resurrection had begun, Jesus being "the
first fruits from those who have fallen asleep," and
the spirit was at work as the prophet Joel had
promised, and the Messiah was now enthroned in
heaven, and one prayed in the Lord's Prayer: let
your will become manifest on earth as it is now
manifest in heaven.—Maranatha.

It may be suggested that this and similar layers
of Christian thought, piety, and experience will
prove significant to keep in mind as we resume

the debate between Judaism and Christianity. No
one could or should claim that such language is
an inadequate witness to Jesus as the Christ. Nor
is it easier to take than much of the later Christological or trinitarian development. But it is a
language cut out of the same cloth as that of
Judaism. And Judaism, in turn, has had its own
developments. Yet one point at which to start is
where the communications broke off, perhaps for
extraneous reasons. This is not to turn the clock
back; that neither should nor could be done. But
since the picture of that early history has been
one of the alienating and agonizing factors in the
later developments of our relations, let us at least
get the record straight. And let us compare similar
things, i.e. first century Judaism with first century
Christianity. To compare Buber to Paul, and Tillich to Akiba or Philo is nonsense from many
points of view. And so it is to compare Jesus to
Maimonides, and Hillel or Qumrân to Origen or
Chalcedon.

7. But what about Paul? In the more recent
phases of Jewish studies of Christian origins there
has been a tendency to recognize Jesus as somehow within the pale of Jewish tradition: Jesus as
one of the great teachers in the prophetic tradition. Such an "Ehrenrettung" of Jesus has usually
taken place at the expense of Paul. Paul the Jewish
renegade is then blamed for having transformed
and distorted the teachings of Jesus into a
sacrilegious hellenistic mystery religion in which
the properly Jewish sentiment of monotheism
yields to claims of the divinity of Jesus. Or we
hear about Paul's willful or inadvertent misunder-

standing of Judaism and its understanding of Law, Mercy, Repentance and Forgiveness.

It is striking that such assessments of Paul depend heavily on an understanding of Paul which was set forth by apologetic and tendential Christian interpreters. In such studies Paul's words and attitudes have often lost their connections with the specific issues which were Paul's primary concern. "Judaism" and "Judaizers" became symbols of self-righteousness and legalism as discussed in the controversies of the Western church by Augustine, Luther, and Harnack. One could perhaps have expected Jewish scholars to be more sensitive to the primary setting of Paul's arguments than were their Christian contemporaries. Only recently, through the work of men like Johannes Munck, have we begun to see more clearly how Paul was positively related to Judaism even in his sharpest arguments in favor of the inclusion of the Gentiles into the people of God. And Paul's doctrine of a justification by faith without the works of the Law was primarily a scriptural argument, according to the exegetical principles of Judaism, in defense of his mission to the Gentiles. It was not a promulgation of a superior religion or of a deeper insight into the nature of grace, superior to that of "benighted pharisaic legalists."

Thus Paul's epistle to the Romans reaches its climax in chapters 9-11, where he gives his most explicit views on the relation between the Jews and the Gentile Christians. He, the apostle to the Gentiles, is not only full of what could have been a condescending concern for his "kinsmen according to the flesh;" as he looks toward the consum-

mation of history, he cannot imagine that end
without the final salvation of the Jews. He goes as
far as to consider the mission to the Gentiles and
the success of that mission in the name of the
Messiah Jesus only as a detour which ultimately
must lead to the point where the Jews accept this
same Jesus as their Messiah. To him this is necessary; otherwise God would not be the God of
Abraham, Isaac and Jacob. He reminds his Gentile
Christians that they certainly have no reason to
boast and to feel superior to the Jews. On the
contrary, they should remember that they are wild
branches, only engrafted on the true olive tree of
Israel. "So do not become proud, but stand in
awe."

It is of interest to note that Paul does not think
about this final return of the Jews to their Messiah
as the result of a mission from the Gentiles. At
least he nowhere admonishes his congregations to
such efforts. Nor does he intimate that it will come
about by a spectacular display of virtue on the
part of the Gentile Christians. In accordance with
his good pharisaic training he looks toward this
return as a mystery which lies in God's hands and
which will happen in God's own time. But without
such an end the gospel could not be the gospel
and Jesus could not be the Messiah.

The Pauline panorama suggests to us and to
our concern for the relations between Judaism and
Christianity that these two are far more closely
connected than we are apt to think when we speak
about them as two religions. It suggests even that
the Gentile Christian is what we might call "an
honorary Jew." As Christians we speak to our
Jewish friends and ask them to consider our claim

to be fellow heirs to their promises. We claim that right by faith in Jesus the Messiah and for his sake. Such a claim appears to be well in accordance with the image which has emerged from our reconsideration of some of the earliest facets of our common and divided history.

Such a view has a strange effect on the present situation. First it reminds us that the New Testament has something to say about our relation to actual Jews. There are many good Christians who know their New Testament and the eleventh chapter of Romans quite well. But, to them, the "Jew" has ceased to be a real Jew; it has become that negative symbol for legalism and self-righteousness. The church has so spiritualized its Scriptures that they have lost their original and concrete meaning. While this at points has a beneficial effect, it has also been impoverishing and misleading. The Vatican Council seems to follow a spiritualizing course when it expresses the conviction that all mankind shares in the guilt of Jesus' condemnation. The validity of such a *theological interpretation* of the gospels can hardly be denied by any Christian. It should become a cornerstone in our catechisms and it will prove highly beneficial. But such an interpretation should not deprive Israel of its particular role in God's history, nor should it absolve the churches from listening obediently to Paul's warnings against Christian boasting and superiority feelings.

What is far more important is, however, the way in which Paul's vision somehow reverses the present sentiment of many Christians. The Gentile Christian now finds himself in need of defending his right and his claim to be one with his

Jewish brother. With that attitude the debate
which was drastically interrupted can be resumed.
For the Christian there is an inner necessity to resume it. Not for the benefit of the Jews but for the
sake of his own faith and identity. And that at the
very center of the faith.

What good could come of such a resumed debate? The history of the debates between Judaism
and Christianity has many chapters which make
such encounters the last thing to be encouraged.
Vestigia terrent. But if the general climate from
which we took our point of departure is what I
think it is, and if the attitude of which we have
just spoken in the context of contemporary biblical
studies is a valid one, then the debate is not only
necessary for the reasons given but holds much
promise. Not that we know where it will lead, but
it should at least bring us to the point where we
differ and disagree for the *right* reasons. In the
atmosphere of the university such a result is a
great and purifying achievement; in the hands
of God it may prove fruitful and significant beyond our planning.

Our plea for such an approach should, however,
never lead us to forget or belittle the unity of our
common humanity. That unity is all the more significant for Jews and Christians since as human
beings we have more things in common than
many: the faith in God, a God who acts in history; the glorious and demanding values of what
could be called the Hebrew-Christian tradition;
with these we share in the common responsibility
to our fellow men near and far. All these things
bind us together in an all-embracing brotherhood
with truly universal ties. And yet the future does

not lie only in the attempts at letting all that is particular to each of us be swallowed up in an ever-growing universality.

It seems that the power of religion in men's lives and in human culture lies in the specific, the particular, i.e. that which divides. Here philosophy and religion part ways and reach their intensity and identity in opposite directions. Worship and faith reach truth and creativity by intensifying the specific, the particular. I guess that is why we are apt to speak about a personal God, and that is why the language of worship must always be closer to myth and poetry than to philosophy. Thus the particular—which is the divisive—is of the essence to our two traditions. We can only proceed by purifying our understanding and intensifying our grasp of the particular, even toward the point of transcending it; and yet we retain the specific, lest those who come after us be deprived of that transcendence.

TORAH
AND DOGMA:
A COMMENT

W. D. Davies

The suggestion has often been made recently
that the relationship between Judaism and Christianity can be adequately described in terms of a
"schism." This suggestion is worthy of serious consideration. It has much to commend it. It promises
new possibilities (badly needed in view of past
history), because "schism" can be healed. But its
mere attractiveness and beneficial potential should
not blind us to the problems involved. Because the
term "schism" presupposes an underlying unity,
its use to describe the relation between the two
faiths preserves an emphasis which, in our given
situation, where the dependence of the church on
the synagogue is not sufficiently recognized, is too
easily lost. And yet, without very careful defini-
tion, the term "schism" may be misleading. Who
are to be called schismatics? Is it Christians for
leaving Judaism or Jews for rejecting the Christian Messiah and his people? As will become
apparent in the following pages, there are two
extreme positions to be avoided. On the one hand,
that which regards the relationship between
Judaism and Christianity at the present time as
so close that that relationship is merely schismatic,

and, on the other hand, that which regards that relationship as one of unrelieved antithesis.

I

The two terms, Torah and Dogma, in this chapter stand for Judaism and Christianity respectively. Such a designation is understandable, but by no means unproblematic. It is important to recognize its implications and limitations. It implies that the characteristic mark of Judaism is *Halakah* or *Torah* and that of Christianity *Dogma*.[1] The one religion is primarily concerned with the "way to live"—*halak*, "to walk"—the other with the way to believe, with the proper creedal formulations.

Now, this distinction between the two faiths cannot be pressed to the last degree. In a limited sense it can be claimed that Judaism demands certain beliefs. Scholars have pointed out a kerygmatic core in the Old Testament. Just as behind the New Testament there is a kerygma centered in an event—the life, death and resurrection of Jesus of Nazareth, so in the Old Testament the Exodus constitutes a kerygmatic core. This emerges clearly in passages where "creedal," confessional materials older than the texts in which they occur break through, as in Deut. 26:5ff., which recapitulates the mighty deeds which gave birth to Israel (see also Deut. 6:20-24; Joshua 24:26-34; Deut. 4:32-34, etc.). The kerygmatic core in the Old Testament is a kind of confession of faith. Again the *Shema* expresses the quintessence of a faith—if you like, a dogma of Judaism. Occasionally in the *Mishnah* an anathema is ut-

tered against those who deny certain cardinal
tenets of Judaism. A famous passage in M. Sanhedrin 10:1 reads as follows:

All Israelites have a share in the world to come, for
it is written, *Thy people also shall all be righteous,
they shall inherit the land forever; the branch of my
planting, the work of my hands that I may be glori-
fied.* And these are they that have no share in the
world to come: he that says that there is no resurrection of the dead prescribed in the Law, and [he that
says] that the Law is not from Heaven, and an
Epicurean. R. Akiba says: Also he that reads the
heretical books, or that utters charms over a wound
and says, *I will put none of the disease upon thee
which I have put upon the Egyptian: for I am the
Lord that healeth thee.* Abba Saul says: Also he that
pronounces the Name with its proper letters . . .
(Danby translation).

Later on Maimonides was to issue his understanding of Judaism as a creed, and nineteenth
century movements in Judaism, both Conservative
and Reform, sought to clarify the tenets of
Judaism.[2] A British author, in a volume entitled
Judaism as Creed of Life, summarizes Judaism
as belief in God and human responsibility. The
point is that there is a "dogma" or "creed" implicit,
if not always explicit, in Judaism.[3]

But, when all this has been granted, the essential demand of Judaism is obedience to the Torah,
the observance of the *Miswot.* The anathemas in
Mishnah Sanhedrin 10 strike one as being hap-
hazard: they are not the considered "dogmatic"
pronouncement of an authorized body of leaders
nor are they presented with the full blasted force

of a "dogma"; they do not stand out in any way from other materials in *Sanhedrin;* they are given no prominence, not to speak of preeminence. Not dogmatic pronouncements, but legal directions are important. The musical "Fiddler on the Roof" opens with a catching song on Tradition. Precariously balanced as Judaism has been on the whims of the Gentile world, what has kept it alive is Tradition—a way of doing things, a way of baking bread, sewing clothes, slaughtering animals, keeping the house clean. Judaism is a way. And the song asks: Whence is this tradition? Who gave it? Nobody quite knows; but it is *here,* and Jews live by it. True, the composer of "Fiddler on the Roof" may be an *am haaretz.* But the song, nevertheless, illustrates the concern of Judaism. The primary concern is not the understanding of Tradition, not the formulating of it by doctrine and dogma, although there is a search for the grounds of Torah, that is, the reasons for the commandments. The heart of the matter is rather living it, observing it, albeit with love, joy and trust in God, the Father.

It agrees with this that within Judaism "belief" can range at will. There are certain implicit, and sometimes explicit, basic principles to which we have already referred. But these apart, it is rightly, if humorously, asserted that where there are three Jews, there can be four opinions. For example, there is no one doctrine of the Messiah. It is easily possible for a Jew to claim to be the Messiah without incurring censure, provided he observes the *Miswot.* Herbert Danby is reported to have once said, playfully no doubt, that he once lectured in Jerusalem when there were six messiahs in his audience. To observe the Law confers freedom for almost anything else and, to parody Augustine, a Jew might urge: "Observe the Law and believe what you like." There was recently, for example, the extreme but interesting case of an American rabbi who refused to believe in God and yet continued in the rabbinate.

Jewish scholars often affirm that what Judaism presents us with is a multiplicity of individual opinions, but no "theology." For example, a distinguished Jewish scholar on reading the chapter in my recent work *The Setting of the Sermon on the Mount,* which deals with the concept of a New Torah, courteously commented that, while all the data in the chapter were correct, he wondered whether one could deal thematically, as I had done, with any idea in the rabbis. The rabbis were individuals holding diverse opinions. Certainly they held certain ideas which were theological, but they were not systematic theologians in any sense; they never construed a theology for Judaism nor any dogmatic system.[4] It is significant that Solomon Schecter wrote a book not on *Rabbinic Theology* as such, but on *Some Aspects of Rabbinic Theology,* a title which suggests the fragmentary, unsystematic character of its theme; and it is often hinted that he had great difficulty in writing even on aspects of it.

Related to this, and perhaps determinative of it, is the fundamental fact that, however much exaggerated by Christian scholars, rabbinic piety is essentially nomistic in that it was the Torah given on Mount Sinai in a past age that was regulative for all life. "The Rabbis," writes Cohen, "would have denied that they were originators

of Jewish thought. All they would have admitted
was that they were excavators in the inexhaustible
mine of the divine Revelation contained in the
Scriptures and brought to light treasures that lay
hidden beneath the surface." [5]

In addition to all the above, another factor
causes many modern rabbinic scholars to hesitate
to formulate a theology of the rabbis, and that is
the unexamined and unsifted character of the
rabbinic texts on which such a formulation would
have to be based. This can best be illustrated, for
example, from the illuminating studies of Judah
Goldin on various key texts. He shows how very
fluid the rabbinic tradition was and how precari-
ous any theological construction built upon them
must be. [6]

The upshot of all this is that there is what might
almost be called a consensus that Judaism is essentially *halakic* and not theological: it is not orthodoxy but orthopraxy that marks Judaism. Judaism
—to use a term that has been used to express this
point of view—is *pan-halakic*. [7]

There are Jewish scholars who hold a different
view. Abraham Heschel has urged that *Haggadah*
can be made to reveal distinct theological currents
of thought within Judaism. He distinguishes a
theological difference between the traditions
emanating from the school of Rabbi Akiba and
those from the school of Rabbi Ishmael, finding
the one more mystical and the other more rational
than the other. [8] Heschel's work is too recent to have
been assimilated and assessed, and it would be
presumptuous on my part to enter into this debate,
but we may point out certain factors that are
pertinent in its evaluation. The implication of

Heschel's position is that in the Tannaitic period
theological speculation of a sophisticated kind prevailed in rabbinic schools. One thing does suggest
considerable speculation at least, even if it were
not systematic, and that is the very great extent of
the haggadic material extant in rabbinic sources.
It is far more extensive than strictly halakic
material. Despite its formlessness, it is difficult
to imagine that such extensive haggadah has
merely a kind of fanciful, homiletical significance,
devoid of all serious theological value. Would the
haggadic materials have survived across the centuries, were merely this the case? Moreover, there
are historical considerations which might have
induced a diminution of theological interest in
Judaism since Tannaitic times. Once Judaism
came to occupy an inferior and despised position
in a world where Christianity was dominant, particularly when it increasingly became confined to
the ghetto, it was natural that it should be over-
awed by the intellectual, no less than by the
material and political, dominance of Christianity.
The very magnificence of the theological achievement of medieval Christendom had an inhibiting
effect on any Jewish theological speculation that
might have arisen. And, later, in the period when
Jewry was emancipated from the ghetto, it was
often understandably dazzled by the new world
into which it entered. The lure and fascination of
European culture often very naturally led to a
neglect of Jewish theologizing. By and large, the
intellectual energies of Jewry were consecrated to
the newly opened, expansive, and insidious secular
interests of nineteenth century Europe, when
assimilation became common. When Jewry did

react "theologically" to Western culture, it was natural for it to do so either in a liberal fashion which, like Protestant liberalism, did not foster theological profundity or in a conservative fashion, which led to renewed concentration on *Halakah*. The neglect of theology by secularized and religious Jews in modern times is historically understandable.

However all this may be, it is probably true to claim that the *dominant* position still among Jewish scholars is that in Judaism not opinion, doctrine, or dogma matter primarily, but practice, observance in trust and joy.[9] The peculiar genius of Judaism is expressed not in creeds, like the Nicene or the Chalcedonian in Christianity, but in a law book, *The Mishnah*. While in certain kabbalistic and mystical circles, which have persisted throughout Jewish history, a speculative, even esoteric, interest constantly emerges, the main stream of Judaism appears not to have taken kindly to this and has preferred to retain a kind of massive *halakic* simplicity, suspicious of speculation and uninterested in dogma. The actuality of obedience to the Torah, not theological interpretation of it, has been the hallmark of Judaism. The Torah is the peculiar property of Judaism: it is its heart. The clean challenge of the commandments *(Miswot)* cuts through all the sentimentality, mysticism, gnosticism, and irrelevance of which, according to some Jews and many Christians, the Christian faith has been guilty. Leo Baeck especially has forcefully set forth the cleanliness of the commandment in Judaism over against the murky religiosity and the irrelevant piety of which Christianity is so often capable.[10]

And it is at this point that Christianity is usually claimed especially to differ from Judaism. "All the Christian objections to Judaism," writes Schoeps, "and the corresponding Jewish replies pale into insignificance before the point of dispute ... which was decisive in the life of Saul of Tarsus: whether the Law has not found its fulfilment and been abolished through belief in the Lord and Savior, Jesus of Nazareth." [11]

Now, the Christianity that emerges in the New Testament is not as opposed to Law as Baeck and other scholars, Christian no less than Jewish, have maintained. In Matthew, and even in Paul, there is room for Law, and for a new commandment in John. The early church often strikes one as a Bible class concerned with halakah. As Stendahl has suggested in his well-known book and more recently in an as yet unpublished paper, there is in the New Testament a halakic Christianity.[12] The earliest Christians among other things were called those of "The Way"—of the Christian halakah. Probably this aspect of primitive Christianity has been neglected for a simple reason. The kerygma has so dominated recent scholarship that the didache, although recognized, has been unconsciously and consciously relegated to a secondary status. This is not the place to assess the role of the kerygma in the New Testament. Suffice that it has too often been rigidly and even wholly separated from the total life of the church and presented as a phenomenon in a vacuum. In fact, the kerygma was one aspect of the life of primitive Christianity embedded in and accompanied by a rich communal life—a "way." This "way" has continued to inform the life of the church throughout the centuries. I am not competent to trace this fact historically in its various forms—in the imitation of Christ and otherwise. But it is safe to hazard the statement that it is witness to the "way" among Christians, and not any kerygma proclaimed, that has most furthered the Christian faith. In any case, it is well to recognize that a complete separation of Judaism as a religion of *Torah* from Christianity as a religion of *Dogma* cannot be justified. Christianity too is a halakah.[13]

But once this be admitted, it has further to be stated at once that, in fact, Christianity in the course of time did develop into a dogmatic system in a way which Judaism did not. I am not sufficiently versed in Jewish history to explain why this is so, that is, why Judaism did not succumb to refined dogmatic speculation as did Christianity. In addition to the historical considerations suggested above, one may hazard the suggestion that the Jewish *Halakah* sufficiently safeguarded the uniqueness of Jewish faith. In the *Torah* Judaism possessed a wall of fire which needed no dogmatic justification to surround and safeguard it, so effective was it. And the most obvious reason why Christianity developed into a dogmatic system is that, as the Palestinian faith, without the benefit of a full-blooded unmistakable fence, such as the Jewish Torah, spread throughout the Graeco-Roman world, it had to define itself over against the various forces that threatened it. The evolution of the New Testament canon, the episcopate and especially in this connection, creed, or dogma, is the response of Christianity to gnostic and other well known pressures. Gradually the church became Hellenized, and with Hellenization came orthodoxy, which culminated in the great dogmatic statements of the councils. *Belief,* not *halakah,* became important. The increasing separation of the church from its Hebraic root in the synagogue meant increasingly the predominance of *Dogma* over *Torah.* I am tempted to think that, along with this separation, the threat of meaninglessness in the church increased. Judaism has always managed to retain a massive awareness of the purpose of God, an awareness that made refined theological speculation unnecessary. Christianity, more exposed to the winds of the world, perhaps, has had to fight more the meaninglessness of things, and this fight is one of the sources of its dogmatic evolution. It had to impose a meaning, a creed, a dogma on meaninglessness in a way the more rooted synagogue could afford to neglect.

Has not the time now come for the church to recognize all this fully and by renewing its contact with the synagogue to restore the balance between *Kerygma* and *Didache, Dogma* and *Torah?*

II

Let us turn to the next point. Broadly speaking only, I have suggested that it is justifiable to think of Christianity in terms of *Dogma* and of Judaism in terms of *Torah.* A concomitant of this is a point which, more than any other, I think, has always impressed me very forcibly. It is the absence in Judaism of a *crippling* sense of sin and guilt. One can hardly turn to any of the Christian classics, from the first century down through Augustine to

Luther and thence to Barth and Niebuhr, without
at times being overwhelmed by the profound sense
of sin which everywhere apparently accompanies
Christianity.

True, the sense of sin is not absent from the
Old Testament, as in the familiar Psalm 139 and
elsewhere. "Can the leopard change his spots?"
is an Old Testament verse (Jer. 13:23). The
Day of Atonement is a central festival of Judaism.
True also that the power of the unconscious in
Freud has been traced to roots in Jewish thought
about the *Yeser ha-ra'*.[14] But by and large it is an
invincible optimism that wells up in rabbinic Judaism. The commandment was given to be obeyed,
and the implication is that man can obey it. Jewish
history presents the most incredible record of
justification for utter despair and yet of the per-
sistence of hope. The evil *yeser* is recognized; the
fall of Adam was momentous in its consequences;
everything is determined. Yes: but free will is
given (cf. *Abot* 3:19). I do not recall any rabbinic
passage where there is a pervading sense of the
miasma of sin or anything like a doctrine of
original sin. Sin is a sore to which the ointment of
the Torah may be applied: significantly the evil
yeser is an impulse, not a condition or state, as,
for example, is sin in Paul. There are, it is true,
passages in the Dead Sea Scrolls which approach
the Christian sense of the *miasma* of sin, but even
here sin is essentially transgression. The air that
Judaism breathes is that of the commandment—
direct, fresh, simple. There is in Judaism, as compared with Christianity, little introspection, little
preoccupation with conscience, for which it has

no word, comparatively little torturing of the soul.[15] Asceticism, for example, is largely alien to Judaism, and is condemned by the rabbis.

How different is the history of Christianity where Sin, with a capital S, has been recognized as "exceeding sinful" from the beginning, where "the bondage of the will" is a familiar doctrine. I suggest that where the "optimism" of the kind that pervades Judaism, despite the tragedies of its history, is dominant, *Dogma* is likely to be secondary. It is the awareness of sin that makes the theologian. *Dogma* develops where there is torture, moral and intellectual. The introspective conscience of the West, which is alien to Judaism, is surely one of the sources of the dogmatic concentration of Christianity. The robust, halakic character of Judaism has not been conducive to theological subtlety, of any systematic kind, at least. The commandment to be done, not the creedal conundrum to be unraveled, has been the central concern of Judaism. I should be prepared to say that the chief differences in ethos between Jewish and Christian life, worship and thought are all coloured by the difference in intensity with which the two religions have wrestled with sin.

III

I move now to the third point. In this discussion it has been agreed that Torah and Dogma are terms that can represent Judaism and Christianity. I assume also that the basic structure of Christianity in most of the New Testament documents is to a great extent parallel to that of Judaism. By and large the Christian dispensation or event was understood as a new Exodus from the realm of slavery to sin, the old Egypt, to the life of a new Canaan. Christianity, it may be argued, emerges as a specific kind of Judaism with a new Exodus and a new Moses and a new Sinai "in Christ." What, then, is the difference between the two faiths? This can be expressed somewhat as follows. Whereas in the complex often referred to as the Exodus, at which Israel's redemption was wrought, Judaism came to place more and more emphasis on the Torah, that is, the demand uttered on Sinai, which was itself a gift, the figure of Moses being a colossus because he mediated the Torah, the church, as it looked back to the new Exodus wrought in Christ, first remembered the person of Jesus Christ, through whom the new Exodus was wrought, and who thus came to have for the church the significance of Torah. This is why ultimately the tradition in Judaism culminates in *The Mishnah*, a code of *Halakot*, and in Christianity in the Gospels, in which all is subservient to Jesus as Lord.[16] What then is the essential dogma that has replaced the Torah of Judaism? As I argued in my work *Paul and Rabbinic Judaism*, it is the claim that the Torah now is Jesus of Nazareth, the Christ. There is a new ultimate in Jesus: the finality of Christ replaces the finality of Torah. To claim that the gulf between Judaism and Christianity is merely a schism is to imply that this new finality can be expressed in terms consonant with Judaism. Can this really be asserted?

The finality of Christ, to judge by the New Testament, can only be established even for Christians in terms of the Torah itself. It is a familiar fact that early Christians searched the Scriptures in order to show that the Torah and the prophets pointed to Jesus. Christianity from the first involved the interpretation of the Scriptures, just as Judaism involved an understanding of them. The interpretation of the Old Testament variously given in the New Testament is governed by the assumption that Jesus is the Messiah. Throughout the New Testament appeal is made to the Old. The life, death, and resurrection of Jesus of Nazareth and the emergence of the church is understood in terms of the Old Testment as its fulfilment. But although the New Testament writers draw upon the Old Testament to illumine what had happened in the gospel, they do not draw on all the Old Testament indiscriminately. There are some prophecies which they ignore and others which they modify. Not all Old Testament expectations were suitable for the events which they were interpreting. The New Testament is not dominated by the Old. It is the gospel itself that provides the pattern for the understanding of the Old: the New Testament interprets the Old in the light of Christ. It does not merely interpret Christ in the light of the Old Testament. To put the matter in another way, the New Testament does not paint a picture of its Lord out of all the colors found in the Old Testament. It used the Old Testament selectively, in a creative way; it rejected some colors and used others in the light of Jesus, the Christ.

And given the Christian presuppositions, this Christological principle of interpretation is convincing—but only given the Christian presuppositions. Recall Scholem's view that Christian exegesis of the Old Testament interprets it against its very grain.[17] That is, it is forced and, therefore, unacceptable exegesis: it imputes to the Old Testament a meaning it never intended. Jewish interpretation, on the other hand, springs naturally from the text itself: it is native, indigenous. The kind of schematization that is found, for example, in Romans 9–11, which Christians have always found illuminating and inspiring in its vast historical and theological sweep, is a falsification of the intent of the Old Testament. The issue of the interpretation of Scripture, both in its wider sweep and in matters of minute detail, has cropped up again and again in Jewish-Christian dialogue and it still does and always will. It will necessarily remain with us because the Christological principle of the interpretation of the Old Testament is implied in most forms of traditional and in all forms of essential Christianity.

And, despite its rejection by Jewry, this implies that Christian thought, Christological and other, can be expressed in categories derived from the root of Judaism, which is the Old Testament. And it is arguable that Jewish categories are, in themselves, sufficient to account for the essentials of later Christian dogma, even that of the Trinity. Daniélou, for example, has sought to show how, right down to the Council of Nicaea, Semitic categories were influential in the formulation of Christian dogma.[18] On this view, Christianity can be regarded as essentially a schismatic branch of Judaism. But is it only this?

IV

This brings me, finally, to the term "schism." Although such a model is attractive and has influenced the creative thinking of men like Rosenzweig and Barth, I would merely ask the question, in conclusion, whether the New Testament itself supports the notion that the relation between Christianity and Judaism is that of a "schism." The New Testament presents that relationship in at least three ways.

First, there are documents in which there is little awareness of any essential break between Judaism and Christianity. Jesus has come as the Messiah, but the essential structure of Judaism has remained virtually unaltered. Acceptance of Jesus does not mean any radical break with Jewish practice or belief. All that has happened to Christianity is that Judaism is now in possession of its long-awaited Messiah, but his advent has not demanded perceptible change. The earliest Christians, Judaizers and Jewish Christians who held this position have left few traces in the New Testament itself, although their presence can easily be discerned moving shadowily behind its pages, especially in the Pauline epistle. But they have left us noncanonical materials of fairly substantial extent. The Christianity which these reveal has been examined anew and given great prominence by Schoeps.[19] He finds Jewish Christianity to have been the chief bulwark in the primitive Church against Marcion and the threat of Gnosticism. That Jewish Christianity disappeared almost without vestige is no indication of its real significance in history. From its point of view, the Christian faith is a reformation or revision of Judaism, involving little radical newness, that is, it is a schism. It is, indeed, merely Judaism with an addendum—Jesus the Messiah. We may agree with Schoeps that the disappearance of

Jewish Christianity may be no criterion for what
it connoted in its heyday, but many have regarded
the disappearance as almost inevitable because it
provided no ultimate raison d'être for Christianity
alongside Judaism.

At the opposite extreme, we find, in certain
documents of the New Testament, the claim that
the relation of Christianity to Judaism is one of
sharp antithesis. This comes to clearest expression
in the Fourth Gospel, where there is a sustained
interpretation of the Christian faith which em-
phasizes that it replaced Judaism. On this view,
Christianity is a revolution which so transforms
Judaism that the latter can be regarded as superseded. It is true that the Fourth Gospel urges that
salvation is from the Jews and uses categories that
are derived from Judaism to expound Jesus' significance, but it does look away from Judaism also.
The newness of the gospel is such that the old
order of the waterpots has given place to the new
wine of the gospel. The quintessence of the Fourth
Gospel's attitude may perhaps be understood in
the story of Mary and the beloved disciple at the
cross (Jn. 19:25–27). Near the cross where Jesus
hung stood his mother, with her sister, Mary,
wife of Cleopas, and Mary of Magdala. Jesus saw
his mother, with the disciple whom he loved
standing beside her. He said to her, "Mother,
there is your son"; and to the disciple, "there is
your mother"; and from that moment the disciple
took her into his home. Mary is the mother of
Jesus. She is now handed over to the respectful
care of his disciple. Her function is over. If Mary
here stands for Judaism, the implication is clear.
Judaism is the aged mother. She is honored and

cherished, but a new order to which she has given birth replaces her. Such is the relation between Judaism and Christianity.[20]

To some, then, the gospel is a revision, if not a radical one, of Judaism; to others it supersedes Judaism as its antithesis. The third attitude is best represented perhaps in Matthew and in Hebrews. It may be expressed in terms of Matthew 5:17: "I came not to destroy but to complete." The immediate context in Matthew concerns the Law, but the attitude can be extended to cover the whole of Judaism. The Christian gospel has brought the intent of Judaism to full fruition. It has not only fulfilled the Jewish hope for a Messiah; it has brought with it a new Temple, a new Law, a new sacrifice, a new people. In all these cases the adjective "new" is meant to indicate not antithesis but fulfilment. What in Judaism was "shadowy," tentative, and preparatory is now fully realized in Christ. Readers of the Epistle to the Hebrews do not need to be reminded of the way in which the theology of that epistle is built upon the theology of Judaism as its "completion."

There is one figure, possibly the major figure of the New Testament, apart of course from Jesus, whom it is difficult to place in any of the categories indicated. Paul has been regarded, particularly by Jewish scholars, but also by Protestants dominated by Luther, as having broken with Judaism in a radical fashion. In particular, Jewish scholars have accused Paul of breaking down the fence of the Torah, and Christian scholars have set his doctrine of "justification by faith" over against the emphasis in Judaism on "salvation by work." But there can be little question that Paul remained throughout his life, in his own mind, within the pale of Judaism. Christ was for him the end of Judaism in the sense not of its annulment but of its fulfilment. By and large, I should classify Paul with Hebrews and Matthew, rather than with the Fourth Gospel. To him, also, Christianity is not the antithesis of Judaism but its culmination.

The New Testament, then, presents us with three main alternatives, only one of which, the first mentioned above, justifies the use of the term "schism." I think it must be clearly recognized that there came a point when the two faiths—conceptually as well as historically—had to part company, radically and not merely schismatically, that is, where Christian dogmatic developments made the gulf between the two religions so deep that the term "schism" becomes inapplicable. As long as Jesus was interpreted in strictly messianic categories and, indeed, in terms of Torah, a merely schismatic relationship between Judaism and Christianity is conceivable. But once Jesus is claimed to be God incarnate, and this is already the case in parts of the New Testament itself, then [21] the Rubicon has been crossed and Christianity stands completely outside the conceivable confines of Judaism, the quintessence of which is expressed in the *Shema.* If Christianity be interpreted kerygmatically in terms of the divinity of Jesus, the Christ, then we must speak of a new religion, not merely of a schismatic emergence. No Christian who has ever engaged in even the slightest discussion with Jews can doubt this. The doctrine of the Incarnation is the Rubicon between the two faiths.

The question then emerges whether essential Christianity can ever be expressed in nonincarnational terms which would lessen the gulf between it and Judaism. There are two possibilities to be considered.

The first possibility is to recognize frankly that there is a viable interpretation of the gospel which does not require the affirmation of the historic creeds, couched as they are in mythological language which needs to be de-mythologized. It would seem that Bultmann, for example, if we are to follow one of his recent interpreters, has in fact given up the great dogmatic formulations of the Christian faith. Thus Ian Henderson writes:

More important is perhaps to ask whether Bultmann's position in the controversy about myths leaves open the kind of Christology we find in the statements of Nicaea and Chalcedon. I do not think it does . . . Now this issue is quite vital. For all signs are that Christianity is going to split on the Christologies of Nicaea and Chalcedon . . .[22]

Because it, apparently, removes the offence of Christology, could Bultmann's understanding of Christianity, then, be acceptable to Judaism, and could it be described as merely a schismatic phenomenon? Apparently so. The Jesus of Bultmann stands within Judaism. But here we are faced with a paradox. While for him Jesus stands within Judaism, Bultmann's understanding of the Christian faith is so divorced from the Old Testament and Judaism that the Jesus he presents is divested of any serious significance for Judaism and is thus, from the Jewish point of view, rendered innocuous. A Jesus who is merely a bearer of the Word and not the Word himself, and especially as the bearer of a Word not fundamentally rooted in Judaism, such as he is for Bultmann, offers no challenge to Judaism as such. In such a view of Jesus the Rubicon between Judaism and Christianity is not so much confronted as by-passed. The theological barrier to a Jewish-Christian *rapprochement* in the dogmatic history of Christianity is thereby obviated, but it is also, from the Jewish point of view, trivialized. The possibility raised by Bultmann's view of Jesus not only raises in an acute form the question whether the dogmatic history of Christianity can or should be reversed, but also whether, if such were the case, it would really interest Judaism.

The other possibility, which is hesitatingly raised here, is that which would interpret Christianity, not in *kerygmatic*, but in *halakic* terms. Let us again raise the question how far Christianity can cease to affirm the historic creeds and yet remain itself. That is, would it be possible to conceive of Christianity adequately not primarily as a way of belief, a creed, but rather as a way of life, as *agape?* It is certain that if Christianity finds the essence of its life in creeds such as those of Nicaea and Chalcedon, there can be no ultimate *rapprochement* with Judaism. On the other hand, could not a halakically oriented Christianity be at home with Judaism or, at least, remain as a merely schismatic aspect of it? The answer to this question also, to judge from the history of the church, would seem to be that even a halakically centered Christianity has had Christological implications that Judaism has not been able to accept. Even so conservatively halakic a figure as

James, the brother of the Lord, was finally unacceptable to Judaism and died a martyr's death.
How much less is any halakic Christianity conceivable in our time!

We seem to be driven to one conclusion. There
is a Christological factor, however expressed, in
Christianity which—to use a phrase borrowed
from Reinhold Niebuhr—is non-negotiable even
with its mother faith, just as there is a centrality
of Torah in Judaism which is non-negotiable.
The dogmatic development of Christianity, in
short, remains as the barrier to reducing the relation between the two faiths to a mere schism. It
is the part of wisdom to recognize this. But this,
in itself, is not the tragedy of the history of the
relations between the two faiths. Rather is it that
the spirit of the *Halakah* demanded by both has
not been more truly pursued by both, so as to
make possible, within their dogmatic difference,
mutual tolerance, respect, learning and even affection. At least the time is long overdue for Christians to recognize that the attempt to overcome
Torah by *Dogma* is long past: its almost total
ignominious failure is evident. This already points
forward the emergence of a new era or at least
new possibilities for Christian-Jewish relations.

[1] By *dogma* I understand a truth necessary for salvation
propounded by an authoritative council or organ of the
church.
[2] This emerges clearly in the recent lectures by Joseph
L. Blau, *Modern Varieties of Judaism* (Columbia University Press, 1966).
[3] Morris Joseph, *Judaism as Creed and Life* (Macmillan,
London, 1903).
[4] A Biblical student cannot but ask whether, by the same

standards Biblical Theology, as it has developed in our time, would ever have been possible.

[5] A. Cohen, *Everyman's Talmud* (1932), 132. See R. T. Herford, *Pharisaism* (1912), chapters 1 and 2; J. Bonsirven, *Le Judaisme Palestinien*, vol. 1 (1834), 248f.

[6] See, for example, J. Goldin on The End of Ecclesiastes: Literal Exegesis and its Transformation, in *Studies and Texts*, vol. iii, *Biblical Motifs*, ed. Alexander Altmann (Harvard University Press, 1966), 135-38.

[7] I owe this phrase to A. Heschel's work, *A Philosophy of Judaism: God in Search of Man* (1955), 323, 328.

[8] Two volumes of Heschel's work on this theme have already appeared (unfortunately only in Hebrew) and another is in preparation; *Torah min ha-shamayim*, vol. 1 (1962), vol. 2 (1965).

[9] How the question is exercising modern Jewry can be quickly gleaned from David Aronson, Faith and Halakah, *Conservative Judaism* 21:1 (1966), 34-48.

[10] See Leo Baeck's chapters on The Faith of Paul, Mystery and Commandment, Romantic Religion, in *Judaism and Christianity*, transl. Walter Kaufmann (1959), 139-292.

[11] Hans Joachim Schoeps, *The Jewish-Christian Argument: A History of Theologies in Conflict*, transl. D. E. Green (1963), 40.

[12] *The School of St. Matthew* (1954; 1968²).

[13] For the justification for most of the above paragraph, see my *The Setting of the Sermon on the Mount* (1964).

[14] See N. P. Williams, *The Ideas of the Fall and of Original Sin* (1927), ad rem.

[15] See my article on Conscience in *The Interpreter's Dictionary of the Bible*.

[16] Much of this formulation I owe to Professor David Daube.

[17] Religious Authority and Mysticism, *Commentary* (November, 1964), 31ff. Contrast with Scholem's view that of a Christian scholar, Gerhard von Rad: *Old Testament Theology*, vol. 2 (1965), 333.

[18] Jean Daniélou, *Théologie du Judéo-Christianisme: Histoire des doctrines Chrétiennes avant Nicée*, vol. 1 (1957).

[19] *Theologie und Geschichte des Judenchristentums* (Tübingen, 1949).

[20] I used this symbolic interpretation in my popular work *Invitation to the New Testament* (1966), 492. The symbolism is suggested by A. Loisy, who is referred to, without specific annotation, by E. C. Hoskyns and F. N. Davey, *The Fourth Gospel* (1947), 530.

[21] On this, see R. E. Brown, Does the New Testament call Jesus God?, *Theological Studies* 26 (1965), 545-73.

[22] *Rudolf Bultmann* (John Knox Press, Richmond, Va., 1966), *ad rem*.

A NEW
SENSITIVITY IN
JUDAISM AND THE
CHRISTIAN
MESSAGE

David Flusser

The Judeo-Christian dialogue—be it conducted in the fashion of ordinary human contact or within the discipline of strict scholarly procedure—suffers often from a disturbing pattern: the two partners not only emphasize the elements and features common to both of them, but find themselves confronted in polarity. This emphasis of polarity may prove convenient for the colloquists. Each can assume a polite vantage ground overlooking the position of the opposite religion, yet feel quite content in the assured knowledge of one's own religion because it now bears none of the qualities which distinguish the polar opposite.

The effect of such a polar confrontation concerning Judaism and Christianity gives the impression that we are dealing here with a philosophic-theological clarification of opposite possibilities of the human spirit, which, in turn, seems to proclaim a profound, universal truth. I call into question, however, if this method can obtain validity, even when we decline to proceed merely along positivist-historical approaches.

Polarization as a method of clarification must lead to oversimplification, and this criticism certainly applies to elucidations concerning the complex relationship between Judaism and Christianity. The very fact that Christianity emerged from Judaism challenges such polarization. Since we have made it our task to confront the two religions and their aspects, I deem it preferable to discuss a problem central to both religions. This method of juxtaposition recommends itself for two reasons. It is apt to demonstrate how we ought to proceed in warranted comparison of the two. Secondly, we contend that such a comparison is meaningful only if we employ serene scrutiny in taking stock of the advantages and disadvantages concerning the problem in point within the context of either religion. Such a method obtains only if we prove capable of rising above the vantage ground of our own particular religion.

At his theophany to Israel, God revealed himself as the unique and just divinity. From this aspect, the revelation constitutes a revolution, the direct divine breakthrough to establish evident contact with the world. The message of justice is a central part of this phenomenon. Although it is true that, e.g., Zeus, as presented to us by Hesiod and Aeschylus, brought concepts of justice into the world when he took power, yet the God of Israel initiated a new era with his iconoclastic exclusiveness and his uncompromising moral will. Israel's religion introduced a new concept of justice, a novel law and an original social order conceived in this justice. This postulate of individual and social justice was not to be limited to Israel only. The Creator of the universe postulates this justice of all his creatures; it was incumbent on all peoples of the world.

The concept of justice which emerges from the Old Testament is not the just regimen of mighty men. It stresses that God cares for the poor and unprotected, for the orphan, the widow and the stranger. The basis of social justice was not to be external power and might, but the awe of God who postulates. We could say that this religion of the Old Testament is a plebian religion.

Even with this restriction, the Jewish religion is and remains a moral religion, in which the principle of justice is indispensable. It is for this reason that the dichotomy of humanity into the just and the sinners assumes such major importance. The challenge of theodicy is recognized as a problem by Judaism. Not only is it so recognized in the book of Job and by the prophets; also later on it preoccupied the minds, as we learn from the "three sects" during the Second Commonwealth. The Pharisees, Sadducees, and Essenes differed, as is well known, on the ways of bringing into concord the ideas of divine goodness with divine providence or even predestination.[1] However, the usual formulation of theodicy bears this coinage: how come that we see at times the just suffering and the sinners successful?

In Christianity also the terms "just" and "sinner" rate significantly, and the idea of attending compensation has not been eliminated. However, in the structure of Judaism this idea is located at the core: the concept that the just are rewarded and the sinners are meted out their desert constitutes the testimonial to its veracity. How else would divine justice manifestly rule in the world?

The latter-day Judaism as well as Christianity did not evolve from the religion of Israel in the

Old Testament, but from the Jewish religiosity that flourished during the intertestamental period. This type of religiosity is no longer identical with the creed reflected in the Old Testament. The investigation of this new type of religiosity can lead us to warranted conclusions only if we pay due attention to the diverse trends and movements within the Judaism of the Second Commonwealth. By encompassing all these data we shall realize that in spite of all the respective shades of difference among the groups and sects, we can, on the one hand, formulate ideas and attitudes, trends and approaches common to them all which, on the other hand, distinguish them all clearly from the world of thought and belief that prevails in the Old Testament.

We cannot deal here with the entire complex of structural changes which the Judaism of the Second Commonwealth underwent. Nor shall we deem it our task now to attempt a historical exposition of this development, or to present chronological pegs for its various phases. We shall confine ourselves to only those points of clarification which bear directly on our topic.

We shall start our investigation with the logion of Antigonos of Sokho,[2] who flourished in the second century B.C.E., prior to the Maccabean uprising:

> Be not like servants
> who serve the master for condition of receiving a reward,
> but be like servants
> who serve the master not on condition of receiving a reward.

I contend that these words would have been rather incomprehensible to any one of the sons of Israel during the Davidic reign. Is there a compensation for good works, or is there none? If there is divine compensation and retribution, and I know there is, how can I act and serve as if the just will not be rewarded by God?

However, even in the days of Antigonos of Sokho, this subtle dialectical introversion of the old simple idea of compensation was apparently not conceivable to many of his own generation or even contemporary students of the academy. It would probably have been considered a dangerous proposition, as we can see from information imparted to us in a legendary report,[3] according to which Antigonos had two disciples, Zadok and Boethos. These two had disciples to whom this doctrine was passed on, and so to the next generation of their disciples, who, in turn, asked themselves: "What did the former generations mean by this? Is it possible that a laborer would toil all day long and not receive his due recompense at the end of the day? Had the former generations been convinced that there is reward in a world-to-come, they would not have taught this way." Apparently there is no reward to be granted in the future world—and thus emerged the sects following Zadok (the Sadducees) and Boethos.

This lengendary report indicates, at any event, that the factual modification of the compensatory idea, as reflected in the logion of Antigonos of Sokho, was not taken at face value. Yet we have to bear in mind that this logion is but *one* expression of a new, profound sensitivity that developed within Judaism, which later on was so much taken for granted that it became a second nature, a sensitivity that, in turn, Christianity took over from contemporary Judaism.

Tradition hands down this logion of Antigonos with the conclusion: "And let the fear (or awe) of Heaven be upon you!" In the days of Antigonos, the awe of God was synonymous with the love of God. This equation can be traced to the doctrines of Deuteronomy, and can be followed up through Ben Sira—who also lived prior to the Maccabean uprising and who writes interchangeably and indiscriminately about the love and the awe of God —up to Rabbi Meir of the second century c.e. However, already in the days of the Second Temple there were rabbis who differentiated; the Talmud [4] lists seven types of Pharisees: the two positive types are the Pharisee of awe (like Job) and the Pharisee of love (like Abraham). The latter typology is the more remarkable when we bear in mind the very significant passage during the "Binding of Isaac," in which Abraham is told (Gen. 22:12): "Now I do know that you are God-fearing."

If we now take into consideration the many references in rabbinic literature that compare the awe and the love of God as superior modes of worship,[5] and find that in the majority of these passages love is rated superior to awe in the service of God, then we must arrive at the following conclusion: the problematic conflict arose at some unknown juncture when an oppositional fraction among the Pharisees brought the charge against the veteran group that they were serving God, motivated merely by dread of punishment and retribution but failing to be devoted to him in un-

conditional love. This superior rating of love over
awe prevailed and took hold upon all Jewish
groups. The date of the oppositional fraction was
approximately contemporary with the first controversies within the school of Hillel, more than a
century after Antigonos. This novel discrimination
and differentiation between love and awe, with
preference for the former, finds its reflection in
the early prayer texts, which contain a plea for
divine assistance in serving him in awe, to which
now "love" was specifically added and even put
first.

In our investigation of the new religious sensitivity within the Judaism of the Second Commonwealth, the conflict between the oppositional fraction among the Pharisees, the love-Pharisees, and
the veteran Pharisees who allegedly confined
themselves to the compensatory idea, is of relevant
importance. The new emphasis on love for love's
own sake, irrespective of any compensation, would
indicate a relaxation of the compensatory doctrine
and perhaps render circumstantial evidence for a
growing discontent and uneasiness over the black-
and-white presentation of good and evil in the
doctrines of the Old Testament. This was the new
Jewish sensitivity concerning divine justice as
manifested in the world.

We have pointed out already that Ecclesiasticus
did not discriminate between serving God in love
or in awe. The same lack of discrimination applies
to the book of Jubilees. There (ch. 36) Isaac is
reported to have addressed his sons Jacob and
Esau before his death:

And love one another, my sons, your brothers
even as a man who loves his own soul (himself),

and let each seek in what he may benefit his
    brother . . .
And I shall make you swear a great oath—
for there is no oath which is greater than it
by the glorious, honoured, great, splendid, wonder-
    ful and mighty
name of him who created heavens and earth and
    all therein—,
—that ye will fear him and worship (serve) him,
and that each will love his brother
with affection and righteousness (justice) . . .

Thus the book of Jubilees is the earliest document for the juxtaposition in Midrash fashion of
two Torah commandments which start with the
word We'ahavta, "you shall love": i.e., you shall
love him, your God (Deut. 6:5); and you shall
love your neighbor (or fellowman—Lev. 19:18).
Since in the provenance of the book of Jubilees no
discrimination was made with regard to serving
God in awe or in love, the author of this testament
of Isaac referred instead to the commandment of
loving God (Deut. 6:5) to another, in his eyes
synonymous commandment: you shall fear him,
your God, serve him and swear by his name
(Deut. 6:13).

Although the author in the book of Jubilees
has equated or substituted the love of God by
awe, he still is the first known proponent of juxta-
posing the commandments of divine and altruistic
love, the "great commandments" that were
preached by Jesus. We have already pointed to
the importance for certain Pharisaic circles of unconditional love in serving God, independent of
any compensatory calculations; we shall attempt
to demonstrate that altruistic social love achieved

the highest value index by being considered the very essence of Judaism during the days of the Second Temple.[6]

We can readily notice from New Testament passages (Mk. 12:28–34 and Lk. 10:25–28) that there was no controversy between Jesus and the rabbis concerning the dual commandment of love, divine and altruistic. Hence we deem it incidental that although this dual commandment is found in contemporary extra-rabbinical Jewish sources,[7] it is wanting in the rabbinic sources that have been preserved.

Just as it was remarkable that certain circles among the Pharisees should elevate loving God above the awe due him, so it was remarkable that during that era of the Second Commonwealth the commandment "Love your fellowman as yourself" should have been singled out of the Pentateuch to serve as matrix and foundation of the entire Mosaic law, particularly when we bear in mind that at that time the complex edifice of directive and restrictive commandments was successfully erected. Even if we should want to disregard these problems, we still would have to contend with a situation in which the biblical commandment of altruistic love could obtain comprehensive and fundamental meaning only if we are ready to view their interpretation of the gallant morality of Old Testament justice in the light of "love." This, in turn, is in itself an exceedingly important symptom of the new religious sensitivity of contemporary Judaism.

Much has been written about this commandment of altruistic love, and much material has been collected to bring evidence of rabbinic humanism; here we confine ourselves to the historical understanding of this concept. We see our task as one where we evaluate the situation in the light of the Old Testament and of nascent Christianity, and where we must explicate the structural pattern of divine justice as comprehended by the Jews.

In the book of Jubilees Isaac puts his twin sons Esau and Jacob under "the great oath" to swear in the glorious divine name that they fear God and love each other. This is predicated upon a verse in the Pentateuch to which Isaac is apparently alluding (Deut. 6:13): "You shall *fear him*, your God/ and serve him/and *swear by his name*." On the other hand, the author of this testament of Isaac was evidently familiar with the concept that the commandment of altruistic love was enforced by a divine oath (Lev. 19:18): "You shall love your fellow man as yourself—I—the Lord!" The words "I—the Lord" were understood to mean that God promulgated this law with the seal and oath of his divine name. This tradition has been transmitted by R. Shimeon ben Elazar (second century c.e.). "This word 'Love your fellow man as yourself' has been proclaimed with a 'great oath': I—the Lord, have created him (your fellow man). If you love him, I can be relied upon to reward you, but if you do not love him—I can be relied upon to visit my judgment on you." [8]

This concept is also significant for introverting the compensatory idea by connecting it with altruistic love. Expected compensation now is not inducive to awe of God, but to the love of fellow men. If you love him, you may rely on divine reward, but if you fail to do so, you will be certain of punishment. Similar teaching is reported of Jesus (Lk. 6:37–38): "Judge not—and you will not be judged yourselves./Condemn not—and you will not be condemned./Pardon—and you will be pardoned yourselves./Give—and you will have ample measure given you: they pour into your lap measure pressed down, shaken together, and running over./For the measure you drag out to others—will be dealt back to yourselves." This logion of Jesus may well be considered to illustrate and reflect the contemporary Jewish concept. The first part of the logion calls to our mind what Hillel used to say: "Judge not your fellow man until you yourself come in his place!" [9]

Let us return to Shimeon ben Elazar's interpretation that this commandment was proclaimed under divine oath of compensation and retribution. This is actually a transformation of a dictum of R. Hanina, the deputy of the priests: "The word (Love your fellow man as yourself), on which the entire world is depending, was proclaimed on Mount Sinai with an oath: If (you) dislike your fellow man whose deeds are evil as your own, I, your God, shall visit judgment upon him who dislikes; and if you love him since his deeds are as right as your deeds, I can be relied upon to bestow my mercy upon you for loving my creatures." [10]

This deputy of the priests, Hanina (apparently an important Pharisee of the first century C.E., who was appointed to control the Sadducee high priest), interprets the commandment (on which the whole world is depending) "Love your fellow man—like yourself" as being determined by your right and wrong deeds in solidarity with him; "like yourself" is taken to mean: he—the fellow man—is one like you.

This exegesis of the biblical passage is older yet than the last generation of the Second Temple, for it can be found already in Ben Sira (27:30–28:7):

Wrath and anger, these also are abominations
And a sinful man clingeth to them.
He that taketh vengeance shall find vengeance from the Lord,
And his sins (God) will surely keep (in memory).
Forgive thy neighbour the injury (done to thee)
And then, when thou prayest, the sins will be forgiven.
Man cherisheth anger against another;
And doth he seek healing from God?
On a man like himself he hath no mercy;
And doth he make supplication for his own sins?
He, being flesh, nourisheth wrath;
Who will make atonement for his own sins?
Remember thy last end, and cease from enmity;
(Remember) corruption and death, and abide in the commandments.
Remember the commandments and be not wroth with thy neighbour;
And (remember) the covenant of the Most High and overlook ignorance.

In this passage, which dates back to about 180 B.C.E., the motivating ideas which we have discussed earlier reappear. The doctrine of compensation teaches that if you are mean or callous to your fellow man, you cannot expect God to love you, for "he that taketh revenge, shall find vengeance from God"—measure for measure.

This passage in Ben Sira alludes to the biblical commandment of altruistic love, in the light of

R. Hanina's interpretation: your fellow man is someone just like yourself! This interpretation, which relates the Hebrew comparative pronoun *kamokha* to the subject rather than to the predicate—"your fellow man who is like yourself," instead of "love him like you love yourself"—is sound and legitimate exegesis that can be corroborated by a number of biblical texts, as Wessely has shown in his commentary on Mendelssohn's translation (with a personal objection to it by the translator). Two recent Jewish philosophers, Herman Cohen[11] and Martin Buber,[12] take this interpretation even as the original intent of this biblical verse. I see in this equation of subject and object—he is like yourself—an ingenious and brilliant heuristic boon for the new religious sensitivity of Judaism at that period of the Second Commonwealth. I deem it important to point out that in this passage of Ben Sira the equality of men (within this context of altruistic love) is demonstrated by reference to our being "flesh and blood (27:31)" and thus we all have our weaknesses and "incline towards evil." Hence it would be absurd to "nourish wrath" and bear a grudge against a fellow man who fails, since he too is only "flesh and blood," which makes us aware of our solidarity with all men.[13]

Besides this egalitarian interpretation "for your fellow man is someone like yourself," there was also prevalent during that era another understanding of this verse Lev. 19:18, which bears indirectly but relevantly on our present investigation. It reveals again this novel religious sensitivity of the age. Enquiring about a pithy summary of Judaism, a prospective proselyte was told by Hillel: "What-

ever is hateful to you, do it not unto your fellow.
This is the essence of the Torah, the rest being
just its corollary; now go and study that!" (b.
Shab. 31a).

Bacher[14] sees correctly in this negative promulgation the biblical commandment: Love your fellow man as (you love) yourself, stressing the comparative pronoun *kamokha* as a regulative modifier
of the predicate: love him in the mode and
measure that you love yourself, which, then, in its
negative or restrictive formula is known as the
Golden Rule: Do not unto others, what you would
not have done unto yourself. R. Akiba and, before him, Jesus call this directive for altruistic love
the "essential" or "great commandment" *(kelal
gadol)* principle of the Torah.

Yet it seems remarkable that Jews of this age
should interchangeably cite the great commandment of altruistic love as a direct exhortation as
well as in the restrictive (negative) formulation of
the Golden Rule, with a preference and pre-
valence in Jewish literature for the latter coinage.
We may find the solution in the vernacular
Aramaic paraphrase of the targum Jonathan Ben
Uzziel (a disciple of Hillel, or at least of this
provenance) on Lev. 19:18: "Love (be kind to)
your fellow man: what you dislike, do it not unto
him." The syntactical structure of this passage has
been rendered in this vernacular by the verbatim
translation of the imperative predicate and the in-
direct object, whereas the comparative pronoun
Kamokha has been paraphrased in a negative
version: do not relate yourself to him with dislike,
for you would not want him to treat you with dislike. This paraphrasing stresses the comparative

pronoun as a restrictive modifier of the predicate, over and against the egalitarian stress of this modifier.[15]

Thus we find the concept of loving our fellow man for better or worse, with his only too human frailties, which we all share, since none of us is perfect, as well as the concept of loving our fellow man with the same interest at heart that we reserve for ourselves, and that whatever we are averse to, we should avoid doing to him. Both these concepts belong to the emerging religious sensitivity of the Second Commonwealth. The typological classification of humanity into the righteous and the sinners lingers on as an often repeated shopworn stereotype. In the egalitarian solidarity of the evolving sensitivity it would no longer be gainsaid that there are no perfect righteous and no completely wicked men—for in every human heart the noble and the base impulse are vying with each other.

The pessimistic doctrine of human nature is not only attested in the Thanksgiving Scroll of Essene provenance, but even the author of IV Ezra, who was close to the Pharisee circle of scribes, laments (3:19f.): "Thou didst bow down. . . . To give Law to Jacob's seed, and Commandment to the generation of Israel. Yet thou didst not remove the Evil from their heart that thy law might bring forth fruit in them."

If this is the spiritual tenor of the age, then it follows quite naturally that the awareness of one's own instability and one's own endeavour to combat the evil impulses evokes sympathy and solidarity with those who yielded to temptation and sin. Such insights into one's own complexity begets an evaluation of virtue and vice quite different from the robust black-and-white presentation of the Old Testament. This psychological sophistication and subtle differentiation leads to a refined sensitivity, which at times even appears paradoxical in the "Pharisee" tradition. A Christian will readily appreciate this Jewish anxiety over the ever-looming danger of sin from such tension in his own tradition. Thus we can understand why, for instance, the Jew from this age on, in contradistinction to the psalms of the Old Testament, does not refer in his prayers to the self-righteous distance between himself and "the wicked." Indeed, the prayers of this spiritual climate bear out that it was inconceivable to present oneself to God as meriting attention and consideration for being good, or righteous, or virtuous, or just— for these qualities are attributes that belong only to God.

The monolithic, unsophisticated doctrine of good and evil disintegrated and left many problems in its wake. These challenging questions have brought forth a prismatic variety of answers.

We ought to bear in mind, however, that the disintegration of the uniform doctrine has not proved to be effective for all time to come. The white-and-black image of humanity and the unsophisticated evaluation were merely kept in abeyance but never sank into oblivion. They resurge at later ages (as occurred simultaneously in the church). Nevertheless, the prevailing Jewish sensitivity came to stay, and it flourished at various levels during the long history of Israel, producing ever-new fruits.

On the one hand, the era under discussion saw

the disintegration of the "gallant" simplicity of the Old Testament world image and its attending evaluation of human conduct, but gained, on the other hand, a more profound and complex understanding of human nature and religious rationale, a more sophisticated relationship between the divine and the human aspects. This development, on account of a "pietist" tendency in contemporary Jewry, produced—out of the Old Testament message of a God just and merciful—vectors towards a genuine humanism.

In summing up this discussion, we arrive at the conclusion that the last era of the Second Commonwealth saw a complex dialectic about righteousness and justice, about the pitfalls of sin and the actual, real human aspect of religious conduct which excludes practically the perfectly good person and the completely abandoned sinner; failure and straying from the godly way of life can be corrected by returning to God and the straight path. Virtue and vice are relative terms in the light of this humanism.

Moreover, we have cited the saying of Antigonos of Sokho, which is as early as the pre-Hasmonean Era. It postulates that one ought to serve God for God's sake without expecting compensation for these modes of worship. We have pointed out that this doctrine may have drawn much contemporary criticism and even charges of heresy. Yet we may assume that in wider circles a certain uneasiness was felt over the time-honored central doctrine of serving God for a compensatory consideration. After all, the message of Judaism seemed to be founded on the concept of a just God who meted out to each and everyone what he deserved for

observing or disobeying the divine commandments. We have also demonstrated that the old
image of human and social affairs no longer cor-
responded to the growing sophistication regarding
God and man.

During the time of R. Abbahu, a contemporary
of Origenes, a humanistic statement more radical
than that of Antigonos had been accepted and
reported in Talmudic tradition (b. Taanith 7a):

> Greater is the day of rainfall
> than the day of resurrection
> for the latter benefits only the pious
> Whereas the former benefits pious and sinners
> alike.

Here we find that the time-honored doctrine of
theodicy, or rather anthropodicy, has been ex-
ploded, just as in the Gospel (Mt. 5:44-47):

> But I say to you: Love your enemies, and pray for
> those that persecute you so that you may be (truly)
> sons of your father who is in heaven. For he makes
> his sun rise on the evil and on the good, and sends
> rain on the just and on the unjust. For if you love
> those that love you, what reward have you?

R. Abbahu observes here in the natural phenomenon of providential rain a kind of temporary suspension with regard to the formalism of
divine, compensatory justice; the resurrection of
the end of days was to represent the spectacular
rewarding of the just, whereas the reviving rain
(a miniature resurrection) deals by egalitarian
nonchalance with the just and the unjust. This

must have been understood as a challenge to the old doctrine.

In any event, the dialectic reflected in these and similar statements demonstrates the intricate struggle within Jewish circles that provides the matrix for discussions in the days of Jesus. Most of the source material which we have cited and enlisted for the emerging new sensitivity regarding the evaluation of the righteous and the sinners were culled from "Pharisee" provenance. The theocentric philanthropism of certain scribal circles, mainly the disciples of Hillel (Beth Hillel), served Jesus as one of the two pillars for his doctrine of love. This theocentric philanthropism did not emerge in Pharisee circles out of some vague humanism, but, as we have demonstrated, it evolved in dialectical transformation out of the biblical doctrines and world image without exploding the boundaries of the Old Testament structure. However, we shall demonstrate that Jesus developed this fundamental attitude of theocentric philanthropism into a profound, paradoxical doctrine.

The second source of Jesus' teaching about the righteousness of God is the doctrine of the Essenes and related groups. It is well known that the Essene concepts of good and evil and of the reward of the just and the punishment of sinners are much more radical than those found in the Old Testament. A certain Persian influence upon these concepts is possible, but the doctrine of double predestination, according to which mankind is divided into the chosen sons of light and the accursed sons of darkness, is not of Persian origin. One cannot escape the impression that this rigorous Essene doctrine of hatred may be a radi-

cal reaction against the new sensitivity of the contemporary Judaism, which emphasized the solidarity of mankind both in virtues and in sins, and
which saw in the commandment of love the real
meaning of Judaism. But is not this new Jewish
sensitivity also reflected in the puritanic approach
of Essene theology? In the Thanksgiving scroll
there is the concept that the flesh, the unredeemed
human nature is the sphere of sinfulness and that
the elect can be saved only by the undeserved
grace of God. The Essene concept of sin is not
primitive and nave, but highly theological. The
biblical command of mutual love is in the Scrolls
restricted to the Sons of Light (1QS i. 9–11) and
is paralleled by the sectarian command of hatred
towards the Sons of Darkness. Thus, it seems that
the Essene theology of hatred is a perverted form
of the new Jewish sensitivity. If so, it is not difficult to understand that the inhuman ethics of the
Essenes could in certain conditions develop into
its opposite, into a very specific humanistic approach.[16]

Essenes hoped that at the end of times the
righteous would be rewarded and the wicked destroyed, but, according to the doctrine of predestination, the rule of wickedness in this world
until the final time of its disappearance is preordained by God. Therefore one must hate the evil
and the sinner, but not oppose them, until the
preordained time of vengeance. ("There shall be)
eternal hatred against the men of perdition, *in a
spirit of concealment,* so as to leave to them
property and the labor of hands, as a slave does
to his master, subdued before him who lords it
over him. So he (the member) shall be a man

zealous for the ordinance and its (relation to the proper knowledge of God's) time, toward the Day of Vengeance so as to do what is (God's good) pleasure in all activities and in all his ruling as He (God) has commanded. And all that is done to him he accepts willingly" (1QS ix. 21ff.).[17] This is the strange ideology of peaceful coexistence according to the Essenes.

The same idea is expressed in another passage in the scrolls: the member of the sect asserts: "I will not return evil to anybody, with good will I pursue man, for with God rests the judgment of every living being, and he is the one to repay man for his deeds . . . And the trial of a man of perdition I will not handle until the Day of Vengeance. But my anger I will not turn away from the men of deceit, and I will not be content until He has established judgment" (1QS x. 17–20).[18]

The passage contains a new ethical attitude that developed in the sect from the command of peaceful coexistence until the Day of Vengeance. This fruitful idea is expressed in the words: "I will not return evil to anybody, with good will I pursue man." Nonretaliation itself is in fact a benefit for the wicked oppressor; thus the subsequent step, well-doing to the sinner, is very natural. If you do not oppose the evil and even "pursue man with good," you have found, so to say, a new method of fighting against wickedness in the present. Although this idea is originally rooted in Essene peaceful coexistence, which is an eschatological concept, the ethics of nonviolence and of goodness toward the enemy have their proper, noneschatological values.

If you pursue your neighbor with good, you

need not love him and you can even hate him, because you can explain your behavior by assuming that by acting thus you do not diminish your wicked neighbor's portion of divine punishment. This is evidently the meaning of Rom. 12:19f.[19] and very probably of the last passage quoted from the Scrolls, but this attitude is prone to develop into a more humanistic position. In the already quoted passage of the Epistle to the Romans we read also: "Bless the persecutors, bless them and do not curse them" (Rom. 12:14). There is a certain tension between these words and the end of the chapter, because if you bless the evil-doers, you cannot fail to hope that your blessings will be accepted by God. Thus Romans 12:14 is not far from Matthew 5:44. When you pray for those who persecute you, you surely do not pray for divine vengeance.

But there is another, more important point: if you overwhelm the sinner by a human approach, you can make him better. This is not a strictly Essene idea, because it does not fit the concept of double predestination, which does not permit a moral improvement of the Sons of Darkness. Thus it is understandable that this idea is fully developed in a book which originates on the fringes of Essenism, namely in the Testaments of the Patriarchs, especially in the Testament of Benjamin. "If anyone does violence to a pious man, he repents; for the pious man is merciful to his reviler, and holds his peace. And if anyone betrays a righteous man, the righteous man prays; though for a little while he is humbled, yet not long after he appears more glorious, as was Joseph my brother" (Test. Benj. 5:4f.). By the undivided love toward the righteous and toward the sinners, the pious man overwhelms the evil in the sinner: "For the good man has not a dark eye; for he shows mercy to all men, even though they be sinners. And though they devise with evil intent concerning him, by doing good he overcomes evil, being shielded by God" (Test. Benj. 4:2f.). The consequence of this overcoming evil by doing good is that the sinner will turn unto good: "And if you have a good mind, then both will the wicked man be at peace with you and the profligate will reverence you and turn unto good, and the covetous will not only cease from their inordinate desire, but even give the objects of their covetousness to them that are afflicted" (Test. Benj. 5:1).

So in the semi-Essene circles, in which the Testament of Benjamin was written, a "pietistic" approach to the neighbor developed from Essene premises. But not all the Testaments of the Patriarchs are written from this attitude. The Testament of Asher is an outstanding example of the Essene doctrine of hatred toward the sinners. According to this document, "to hate the merciful and unjust man, this, too, has a twofold aspect, but the whole work is good, because he (this pious man) follows the Lord's example, in that he accepts not the seeming good as genuine good" (Test. Asher 4:3). You have to "follow the truth with singleness of face" and not be "double-faced" (6:1f.). A man who is undivided in his love for the righteous and in his hatred for the sinners follows God, who does not accept the seeming good as the genuine good. This is in accordance with the dualistic morality of the Essenes.

This attitude could not be accepted by the "pietistic" semi-Essenes, because these circles applied the Essene doctrine of love also to the sinners and understood the Essene idea that you have to overcome evil by doing good in the light of the precept of universal love. The opposition toward the doctrine of hatred is expressed in the following words of the Testament of Benjamin (6:5f.): "The good mind has not two tongues, of blessing and of cursing, of hypocrisy and truth, of poverty and of wealth; but it has one disposition, incorrupt and pure, concerning all men. It has no double sight, nor double hearing; for in everything which he does or speaks or sees, he knows that the Lord looks on his soul . . . And . . . the works of Beliar are twofold, and there is no singleness in them."

Here we have the Essene precept to be complete and undivided, used in an opposite sense to that in the Testament of Asher. According to this document you have to be single-faced both in your love and hatred, and if you act so, you imitate God. According to the Testament of Benjamin you have to be undivided in your all-embracing love toward all, righteous and sinners; in this you will be different from the works of Belial, because they "are twofold, and there is no singleness in them." A similar idea was also expressed by Jesus: "Love your enemies and pray for those who persecute you, that you may be sons of your Father in heaven: he makes his sun rise on the evil and the good and sends rain on the just and the unjust . . . You must be perfect as your heavenly Father is perfect" (Mt. 5:44–48).

We have seen that in the semi-Essene circles

there was an inner development from the Essene "peaceful coexistence" toward the teaching of undivided love, and it is therefore clear that those circles came very near to such Pharisees as saw in the precept of love toward the neighbor the essence of the Law and thought that to love God is better than to fear him. Thus, it is easy to understand why the semi-Essene circles were prepared to accept these two teachings. As we have tried to prove in this article, the Great Commandment of Jesus is according to the spirit of certain Pharisaic circles; therefore, as we have said, it is strange that the midrashic combination of the two biblical verses, speaking about the love of God and the love of neighbor, is not preserved in rabbinic literature. We know this sublime midrash only from the mouth of Jesus—and from the semi-Essene literature, namely from the Jewish "Two Ways," [20] and from the Testaments of the Patriarchs.[21]

It is imperative to see the central importance of eschatology in Jesus' teaching, but if we analyze his moral doctrines from a noneschatological point of view, we can see similar ideas both in the semi-Essene trend of Judaism and in such trends of Rabbinism as are strongly imbued with the attitude of what we have called the new Jewish sensitivity. We mentioned the fact that the Essene theology of hatred developed in the semi-Essene circles into a theology of undivided love so that it could be influenced by the moral attitude of the "Pharisees of love." It is therefore possible that even these "rabbinic" elements were accepted by Jesus from the semi-Essene circles known to us from the "Two Ways" in the Didache and the

Testaments of the Twelve Patriarchs. Although this possibility exists, we have to be cautious, not only because the "rabbinic" elements in Jesus' preaching are so strong and typical for him that a secondary influence seems less likely, but also because religious movements are of a complex nature.

But even if it seems probable that the moral doctrine of Jesus is influenced both by the semi-Essene "pietism" and the "rabbinic" sensitivity, it is clear that Jesus' moral approach to God and man, even in points which are possibly influenced by others, is unique and incomparable. Let me mention only one aspect of Jesus' sublime teaching. The old Jewish theodicy—or anthropodicy—is weakened both in "rabbinic" and in semi-Essene thinking: your approach to the righteous and to the sinners shall not be dictated by your love and hatred. According to the teaching of Jesus you have to love the sinners, while according to Judaism you have not to hate the wicked. It is important to note that the positive love even toward the enemies is Jesus' personal message. We do not find this doctrine in the New Testament outside of the words of Jesus himself. But later in Christianity Jesus' doctrine of love became important and cannot be forgotten even by those who do not live according to it. The consequence of the doctrine is today that a Christian knows that you must not make a difference in treating your neighbor according to his moral qualities or his good or bad attitude toward you. In Judaism hatred is practically forbidden but love to the enemy is not prescribed.

Jesus' precept of love is both historically and theologically connected with the fact that the Judaism of the Second Temple period abandoned the gallant idea of righteousness of the Old Testament. It is therefore interesting that with the exception of Matthew—and one verse in Luke (1:75) —the very word righteousness is not found in the synoptic gospels, and in Paul's teaching righteousness and justification means mainly God's undeserved grace toward man. This contributed to the fact that in early Christianity, as it seems, the original concept of Jewish righteousness both of God and of men is even more weakened than in the Judaism of the same period. It is also true that Christianity did not develop a specific Christian concept of social righteousness. It did not need it, at least until Christianity became a state religion, because it possessed its attitude of love and the deep theology (or theologies) of sin, sinfulness, and divine grace. But, from the time of Constantine until today, when Christianity became the established religion of states and societies which themselves did not originate from basic Christian concepts, a Christian answer to problems of justice, crime and punishment, and forensic morality were badly needed. Thus, Christianity always turned in such situations for help to Old Testament or Greco-Roman solutions.

As has already been said, Christianity surpasses Judaism, at least theoretically, in its approach of love to all men, but its only genuine answer to the powerful wicked forces of this world is, as it seems, martyrdom. There is both human greatness and human weakness in our religions, but there is also the common hope for the kingdom of heaven.

[1] See D. Flusser, Pharisees and Stoa According to Josephus, in *Iyun* [Jerusalem] 14 (1964), 318-29 [Hebrew].

[2] *Aboth* I. 3.

[3] *Aboth de Rabbi Nathan*, ed. S. Schechter (New York, 1945), 26.

[4] JBer IX, 14b.

[5] See A. Büchler, *Studies in Sin and Atonement* (London, 1928), 122-30.

[6] See, e.g., W. Bacher, *Die Aggada der Tannaiten*, I (Strassburg, 1903), 4f.

[7] In the "Two Ways" in the *Didache*, *Test. Dan* 5:3, *Test. Iss.* 5:2, 7:6, cf. *Test. Zeb.* 5:1. See also F. M. Braun, Les Testaments des XII Patriarches, *Revue Biblique* 67 (1960), 531-33.

[8] *Aboth de Rabbi Nathan*, 64.

[9] *Aboth* II. 5.

[10] *Aboth de Rabbi Nathan*, 53 (second version).

[11] *Der Nächste* (Berlin, Schocken, 1935), 17. Cohen did not want to decide the philological implications.

[12] See now Hans Kosmala, Martin Buber, *Annual of the Swedish Theological Institute* 4 (1965), 13-17.

[13] See also Sir. 18:13a. To the text see R. Smend, *Die Weisheit des Jesus Sirach erklärt* (Berlin, 1906), 165.

[14] See note 6.

[15] In the Targum Jonathan of Lev. 19:34, the Hebrew *kamocha* is explained in the same way.

[16] The following pages are based upon the important article of K. Stendahl, Hate, Non-Retaliation, and Love, *Harvard Theological Review* 55 (1962), 343-55.

[17] Stendahl's translation.

[18] Stendahl's translation.

[19] See Stendahl, *op. cit.* The whole passage (Rom. 12:8-21) contains motifs known from the Dead Sea Scrolls.

[20] *Didache* 1:2.

[21] *Test. Dan* 5:3; *Test. Iss.* 5:2; 7:6; cf. *Test. Zeb.* 5:1 and Jub. 36:7f.

THE
PROBLEM
OF DIALOGUE
BETWEEN JUDAISM AND
CHRISTIANITY

Manfred H. Vogel

One hears a great deal about the desirability
and the need for a dialogue between Jews and
Christians. In this connection it is often observed
that it is the Christian who on the whole is eager
to initiate and enter the dialogue, while the Jew,
on the other hand, is by and large passive, silent
and even reluctant, although a growing openness
and readiness can be detected of late in some
quarters. Accepting this observation as a basically
accurate portrayal of the situation, we will attempt here to discover and analyze some of the
factors—theological, historical, social or psychological—which may help to explain these differing
attitudes of Christian and Jew toward the dialogue. We want to understand *why* the Christian
"on the whole" and the Jew "by and large" adopt
these attitudes toward the dialogue.

Underlying this attempt is the conviction that
the differing attitudes of Christian and Jew toward
the dialogue are not arbitrary or dependent on
contingent, extraneous circumstances, but are essentially the expressions of the dialogical orientation of their respective faiths. This conviction can
be substantiated if we can show that it is indeed

Christianity and Judaism themselves which manifest these dialogical attitudes ascribed to their adherents. It is Christianity, and not just the Christian, which is on the whole eager to initiate and enter dialogue; it is Judaism, rather than just the Jew, which is by and large passive, silent and reluctant.

How do we account for these differences? What are the factors that are conducive to a dialogue, whose presence is necessary for a dialogue to take place? We submit that there are two factors, both of which must be present in order for a dialogue to take place: kinship and difference.

No dialogue will take place between two parties who lack all kinship, for it is kinship that involves the two parties in each other, thus providing the matrix, the common ground, in which the dialogical movement can occur. Without kinship the two parties are isolated islands without any bridge to connect them, knowing little about each other and caring even less. But kinship, while it is a necessary condition, is not sufficient for the dialogue to occur. Kinship requires a note of difference which will provide—by introducing the issue or issues separating and delineating the parties—the trigger which initiates the dialogue. Without it, one may have a monologue but not a dialogue. If all we can do is to totally agree we might as well talk to ourselves. But just as kinship functions dialogically only when accompanied by difference, so difference, if it is to be dialogically effective, requires kinship. For only against the background of kinship does difference assume importance and significance. Indeed, the more intimate the kinship is the more disturbing and significant does the difference become. In the last analysis, therefore, it is the tension which is produced by the presence of both which is the necessary and sufficient condition for initiating and maintaining the dialogue.

I

How is one to explain the dialogical attitude of Christianity toward Judaism? In order to answer this question we must introduce (or as some would prefer to say abstract) the distinction between two major trends which, although radically different from each other, nevertheless exist side by side within Christianity: the trend which is grounded in the Hebrew Bible and which therefore understands Christianity in the categories of the Jewish thought-world of the Bible and early post-biblical Judaism, and the trend which is grounded in Hellenism and which consequently understands Christianity in the categories of the pagan thought world of Hellenism and its neo-Platonic philosophical articulation. Christianity's attempted synthesis between these two thought worlds would seem to have succeeded only in holding both thought worlds within its grip (by using the same basic terminology, e.g., Messiah-Christos, and attaching both trends to the figure of Jesus) rather than in authentically unifying and harmonizing them. But regardless of how successful in the last analysis we view the synthesis as a whole, in trying to analyze and understand the dialogical attitude of Christianity toward Judaism the distinction between the biblically grounded trend and the Hellenistically grounded trend should prove very helpful.

In the biblically grounded trend within Christianity we find that the dialogical factors of kinship and difference inhere in its very essence, thus giving it a continuous impetus to seek a dialogue with Judaism. The factor of kinship lies primarily in its tendency to view Judaism as its source and origin. The very essence of the Christian message here is contingent upon the acceptance of Judaism as the origin. For biblically grounded Christianity sees itself as the "fulfillment" of the "promise" of Judaism. The "promise" of Judaism must therefore be accepted into the Christian scheme of things as an organic and integral part: the "fulfillment" is contingent upon accepting the "promise." The fact of origin, therefore, is not a mere chronological datum of temporal precedence. It participates in the very essence of Christianity. Judaism as origin provides biblically grounded Christianity its thought world. It provides it with the basic understanding of the scheme of things, the nature and meaning of history, the essential grasp of humanity in its predicament and its hope for salvation. Indeed, only because of a common world view shared with its Jewish source can the claim of "fulfillment" and the acknowledgment of "promise" be intelligible. The acceptance of Judaism as origin thus establishes from the point of view of biblically grounded Christianity a strong feeling of kinship with Judaism which prepares the ground and makes possible a search for dialogue with it.

Furthermore, Judaism is the *only* origin that biblically grounded Christianity acknowledges. The relation to the origin is here unique, lending added impact to its dialogical effectiveness. Thus, for example, the dialogic value of the relation to

Judaism as origin will not be weakened or minimized when Christianity reaches out to other religions or world views. It remains a relationship which is of a totally different order than the relationships which biblically grounded Christianity may or may not have with the other religions of the world, e.g., Islam or Buddhism, and cannot be compared or put on the same level with them. Nor will the dialogical importance be diminished by the relative weakness of Judaism and the fact that it does not belong to the "big league" of power religions. The origin remains origin even if it fails to acquire power and magnitude, its dialogical significance lies in the kinship that it provides, and this is inherent in the very structure of the relation irrespective of such external considerations as power or magnitude.

But, as already noted, the factor of kinship, although necessary for the dialogue, is not sufficient. A factor of difference must be introduced in order to trigger and give impetus to the dialogue. This is provided by the break that exists between Christianity and Judaism. Biblically grounded Christianity must accept its relation to its origin as a broken relationship. Judaism did not accept Jesus as the "fulfillment" of its "promise." The factor of difference is this, that biblically grounded Christianity exists in a *broken* relation to its origin.

The full force of the break as a dialogical factor for biblically grounded Christianity can be seen by further examining the following. First, because the relation of biblically grounded Christianity to Judaism is unique, the break of this relation, i.e., the rejection of Jesus by Judaism, is also unique.

The rejection of Jesus by Judaism presents, therefore, a totally different situation from the non-acceptance of Jesus by other religions and their adherents. Here, Christianity must inevitably ask: "How is it that the people in whose midst and for whose sake (at least originally) Jesus appeared, have not accepted him? How is it that the people who were first chosen by God to witness his presence and glory, to deliver the 'promise,' were not made to participate in the 'fulfillment' of the witnessing? How is it that the people who were most suited and likely to accept him—because of their past history and vocation and because of the directness and immediacy of their confrontation with Jesus—did not accept him?"

A whole theological apologetics was built by biblically grounded Christianity to answer these questions. In spite of this the Jewish refusal to accept Jesus remains a disquieting and disturbing factor to Christianity. It would seem that no matter how convinced it appears to be that it has the solution to this perplexing phenomenon, deep in its heart uneasiness persists. This is really quite understandable, for here, after all, the very essence of its commitment is at stake, since it must take seriously and concretely the historicity of the coming of Jesus. Biblically grounded Christianity, therefore, can have no rest till the Jewish people who are the people of the "promise" have accepted the Christian claim to have "fulfilled" the "promise." Hence, biblically grounded Christianity is constantly driven toward dialogue with Judaism in the hope of finding the answer or of overcoming the rejection.

In the desire and hope to overcome the rejec-

tion, however, resides the danger of vitiating dialogue by transforming it into a strategy of conversion. Authentic dialogue lies in freedom from
ulterior motives in meeting your *begegner*. It resides in offering yourself to the other wholly and
authentically as you are and accepting and listening to the other as he is as an end in himself. Any
manipulation of the other, any use of the meeting
as a means to another end is vitiating. Authentic
dialogue can mean only self-clarification, not the
settling of an argument by winning the *begegner*
to your side. It must preserve, strengthen and
realize the I and the Thou who enter the meeting.
In the desire and hope to overcome the rejection
lies, therefore, the imminent danger of reducing
the *begegner* to an object-for-conversion. On the
other hand, however, if in the hope for conversion
an authentic part of the Christian's being is expressed, then it would be equally vitiating to the
authentic dialogue to forbid the Christian *a priori*
to express that hope. If one may not transform
the other into an object conforming to his interests
the other may equally not mold the one by exclu-
sions and restrictions into an object appealing to
his desires. So it would seem that both the exclu-
sion and the inclusion of the Christian hope for
the conversion of the Jew may vitiate the dialogue. The answer to this dilemma seems to us to
lie in the manner in which the hope for conversion
is expressed, and the role it plays in the dialogue.
The mere confessing of the hope may well be required for the dialogue to be authentic. But when
hope becomes the end which determines dialogue,
indeed, which motivates the Christian to enter the
dialogue, then it is vitiating. The line between the

two roles that the hope for conversion can play in the dialogue is evidently very fine. Here lies the danger that the Christian may slip almost unknowingly from the authentic role to the vitiating one.

Second, the break is an extremely strong factor of dialogical orientation because the self-understanding of biblically grounded Christianity as the "fulfillment" of Judaism holds that this "fulfillment" is the *final* and *ultimate* "fulfillment" since the "fulfillment" here is based in a messianic claim. It is authenticated not by any human claim, which would necessarily be finite and provisional, but by him who is by his very essence final and ultimate. Only in the light of such a claim can one fully understand why the Jewish nonacceptance of Jesus is such a nagging and central problem for biblically grounded Christianity. It is the absoluteness of the claim that the Messiah *did* come that makes the continuous existence of the Jewish people apart from Jesus such a problem. Precisely because the Christian claim is absolute and final, it cannot let the Jewish nonacceptance of Jesus rest. Christianity cannot wait patiently till the time comes when things are clarified. If the Messiah did appear and the Jewish people did not accept him, there is no future to await. Consequently biblically grounded Christianity is continuously propelled from within itself to seek the dialogue in order to clarify things in the present.

Third, the break is further strengthened as a dialogical factor by the fact that when viewed from the standpoint of biblically grounded Chris-

tianity, it does not mean a rejection of Judaism.
Had the break signified a rejection of Judaism, it
would have meant the close of any openness toward the dialogue. Rejection would have expelled
Judaism from the consciousness and concern of
Christianity. It would have signified the end
rather than the beginning of the dialogue. But
biblically grounded Christianity has never rejected Judaism. On the contrary, it intends to fully
accept and incorporate Judaism into itself. It only
claims to "fulfill" and transcend Judaism. The
break is caused by the something extra which
biblically grounded Christianity wants to add to
Judaism, not to substitute for it. Judaism remains
an integral and, indeed, a necessary part of the
total picture, since it is the necessary prologue in
the drama of salvation without which the climax
which Christianity has come to proclaim would
not be possible. Thus, while biblically grounded
Christianity differs from Judaism, it holds Judaism
firmly and persistently within its grip. In such a
context the break is most definitely dialogically
oriented.

Fourth and finally, the break is strengthened as
a dialogical factor by the fact that although biblically grounded Christianity incorporates Judaism
into itself, it is nevertheless the party which in
the last analysis is responsible for initiating the
break. Christianity introduced the new claim that
led to the break. Judaism may have indeed final-
ized the breaks by not accepting this new claim,
this new testament, but it did not initiate it. Christianity, not Judaism, broke away. He who breaks
away has the psychological need to enter into dia-

logue with his origin so that he may present his
case, justify his break, establish his cause and
thus secure his self-integrity and identity.

Thus, the factor of the break is itself constituted
of a dialogical polarity. It is a break, yet not a
rejection. It is at once an act of transcendence and
an act of inclusion. Biblically grounded Christianity in its relation to Judaism is, therefore, thoroughly dialogically oriented. This is of the very
essence of its consciousness.

The dialogical situation between Christianity
and Judaism changes radically when one comes
to consider it from the viewpoint of the Hellenistically grounded trend within Christianity. In
this perspective the factor of kinship, which so
essentially characterizes and determines the structure and consciousness of biblically grounded
Christianity, is missing. Consequently, the relation
is determined almost exclusively by the factor of
difference. And since the factor of kinship is missing here, the relation of Hellenistically grounded
Christianity to Judaism cannot be dialogically
oriented.

Of course, Hellenistically grounded Christianity
cannot escape the fact that as a matter of history
Christianity first arose in ancient Palestine in the
midst of the Jewish people. This, however, is
greatly minimized and assigned peripheral significance only. In contrast to biblically grounded
Christianity, it remains for it a brute historical
event which cannot be denied but which is deprived of any essential meaning.

That Hellenistically grounded Christianity can
so minimize, if not indeed completely ignore, the
significance of its historical origin is due to the

fact that its thought world is the a-historical Greek and not the historically oriented Jewish world view. Concrete history is not the realm in which meaning is unfolded. Its world of discourse, being Greek, is in terms of transhistorical eternal, conceptual verities; at best, concrete historical events are but symbolic pointers. It lives in the eternal present, offering its salvation in that which transcends time and history altogether. In such a context past and future have no organic, essential meaning and significance and consequently the historicity of Jesus and the origin of Christianity within Judaism are only peripheral and essentially meaningless to its structure and consciousness.

This means that not only is the sense of a relation to its Jewish origin greatly weakened but that the common world of discourse with Judaism is practically nonexistent for Hellenistically grounded Christianity. Only because its adopted spiritual origin is the a-historical Greek thought world can Hellenistically grounded Christianity push aside as indifferent its historical beginnings within Judaism. It bears a kinship to the Greek thought world but not to Judaism.

Without the factor of kinship Hellenistically grounded Christianity lacks the common ground and intimacy with Judaism which are necessary to a dialogical orientation. Without this special relation, Judaism becomes just another religion among the many other religions of the world. In fact, when so viewed Judaism lies at a far-removed extreme of the spectrum; it is a religion which is the least likely to elicit an interest leading to a dialogic confrontation. Power or magnitude, which might elicit an interest because of their strategic significance in terms of institutional "power politics," are completely lacking in Judaism. But even more important, the context, concern and orientation of the thought world of Judaism are now at the opposite end of the pole from that of Hellenistically grounded Christianity. The Greek thought world in which Hellenistically grounded Christianity has embedded itself is totally estranged from the thought world of Judaism. Having transferred its special kinship from Israel to Greece, Hellenistically grounded Christianity not only removes a positive dialogical factor but actually introduces a strong negative factor which blocks any dialogical orientation. Its thought world is alien and antagonistic to Judaism. Thus, Hellenistically grounded Christianity would sooner seek a dialogue, as indeed it does, with other religions, as for example the religions of the East (Buddhism or Hinduism), than with Judaism; for the thought world of Hellenistically grounded Christianity is much more congenial to their thought world than it is to that of Judaism. The best that could be expected is that Hellenistically grounded Christianity and Judaism should ignore each other. More likely, antipathy and hostility would mark their relationship.

We may now conclude that on its side the involvement of Christianity as a whole in a dialogue with Judaism at any given time is contingent on the balance between the Hellenistic and biblical groundings in its thought at that time. The more Hellenized Christian thought is, the less dialogically disposed it is; the more biblically oriented Christian thought becomes, the more dialogically disposed it will be. Since the tension between the Hellenistic and biblical poles always exists within Christian thought, its dialogical orientation toward Judaism is a question of degree. "To what extent," one must ask, "is Christian thought, in a given instance, oriented toward one pole or the other?" Following this we may ask: "How involved is Christian thought in the dialogue with Judaism?" Quite evidently the answers will not be all-inclusive and total but qualified by such phrases as "on the whole" or "to a considerable extent."

In recent years it would seem that Christian thought, on the whole, has been moving markedly toward the biblical pole. At the same time, Christian thought in recent years has shown, to a considerable extent, great eagerness to enter the dialogue with Judaism. The connection between the two seems to be unmistakable: the eagerness of contemporary Christian thought to enter the dialogue is the result of this growing biblical orientation.

II

How is one to explain the dialogical attitude of Judaism toward Christianity? Using the same analysis that we have applied in our attempt to explain the Christian dialogical attitude we will show that the necessary dialogical conditions which operate in biblically grounded Christianity are either missing from, or considerably weakened within Judaism. The two basic factors within biblically grounded Christianity which spurred it toward a dialogue with Judaism, its unique relation to Judaism as the origin and the break with Judaism, are either completely absent or greatly minimized in Judaism.

Quite evidently the relation that exists between Judaism and Christianity when viewed from the standpoint of Judaism is no longer, as it was in the case of biblically grounded Christianity, a relation to one's origin. Moreover, Christianity cannot even claim uniqueness in the sense of being the sole offspring of Judaism. Other religions have claimed Judaism as their origin. Nor is Jesus the only one to arise from within Judaism to claim the office of the Messiah. Christianity is but one of a number of religious movements which originated within Judaism, but which Judaism could not accept as the authentic "fulfillment" of its expectation. Nor can Christianity claim uniqueness in the less significant dimensions of power and magnitude. The worldly power and success which Christianity has achieved are, despite its impressive record, not unique. Islam can equally claim worldly success, power, and dominion. Thus, the dialogical factor of kinship in both its aspects, i.e., that of the relation to the origin and that of uniqueness, is cancelled out when the viewpoint is reversed.

The second factor—the break between Judaism and Christianity—when viewed from the Jewish standpoint, also fails to act as a dialogical factor. This is true because the break is deprived of those very characteristics that made it so effective a dialogical factor in the case of biblically grounded Christianity. First, the break with Judaism no longer signifies the addition which transcends but also includes. It signifies Judaism's *total* rejection of that which is distinctly Christian. Nothing in Christianity that is new and lacks a counterpart in Judaism is accepted by Judaism. From the standpoint of Judaism, the break signifies a total lack of contact with the other party. Consequently, it excludes any common ground or note of kinship which could have provided the tension necessary to initiate the search for a dialogue. A break, however, that places the other party so completely outside its field of concern and consciousness burns all bridges. Total rejection signifies total indifference. After the break Judaism remained alone with itself.

Second, the break with Christianity, from the standpoint of Judaism, does not signify the rejection of a Messiah: it is the rejection of a "false Messiah." It is the rejection of one who, no matter how noble and spiritual he may have been, is a man and nothing more. The centrality and importance, therefore, that must necessarily attach to the rejection of a messianic claim are missing. But since the rejection does not occupy a central place in Jewish consciousness, its dialogical force is correspondingly greatly reduced. Moreover, the rejection of Jesus has a finality in Jewish consciousness. True, it is not final in the sense of asserting ultimate validity for the decision. (Indeed, this would have been a messianic claim, the very claim which is rejected here.) It is, however, final in the finite human context of settling the claim for the time being till a messianic claim is accepted, thus removing it for the duration from Jewish consciousness. Consequently, Jesus' claim is no longer a continuously nagging and disquieting problem which must persist and demand reconsideration as long as the claim remains unaccepted. Being a human claim, the case can be closed once the decision is made. Such finality is, of course, a serious block to a dialogical orientation. Without openness to the claim of the other party, interior thrust toward the dialogue is removed.

On the basis of this analysis we can, perhaps, understand now the "silence" of Judaism toward dialogue with Christianity. But we have shown only that Judaism is "silent" with regard to the *initiation* of the dialogue. The analysis does not show that Judaism cannot respond to the dialogue once it is initiated by the other party. To initiate such a dialogue the primary need is to introduce the factor of kinship, for it is the lack of this factor that is the main obstacle. This, however, can be done only by Christianity and only to the extent that it can establish kinship on the grounds of Judaism, for the problem with the dialogical orientation of Judaism, as we have seen, is precisely its inability to find within itself the factor of kinship to Christianity. Thus, if kinship is to be established it will have to be established by the other party. Only to the extent that the other partner to the relation is, so to speak, "Jewish" is the factor of kinship reestablished and the possibility of the dialogical orientation opened. If this can take place there is no reason why a response from Judaism could not be forthcoming.

There are two points which, taken properly, can provide kinship with Judaism. The first is the historical fact that Christianity arose in ancient Palestine while the second is the thought world of Judaism. Evidently, whether these aspects establish kinship with Judaism or not is in the hands of Christianity. For it is up to Christianity whether the brute historical fact of its rise in ancient Palestine is taken to signify a relation to the unique origin or not, and whether the thought world of Judaism is appropriated or not. Judaism cannot make itself significant for Christianity nor can it impose its thought world on Christianity. Judaism must wait for Christianity to take the initiative and turn itself toward it. Christianity can do this to the degree that it understands itself on its biblical grounds, for it is biblically grounded Christianity which is, so to speak, "Jewish." The more biblically oriented, therefore, Christianity becomes, the better are the prospects that Judaism will respond.

This conclusion—coupled with the fact that Christianity in recent years has been moving toward the biblical pole—may account for the fact that a growing openness and readiness may be detected in some quarters of Judaism. Indeed, it is probably true that much of the contemporary Jewish involvement in the dialogue is in the nature of response, i.e., the response of Jews who sense a newly hospitable climate in which Christianity has a sympathetic, appreciative and understanding ear capable of listening to Judaism.

Still, it would be false to conclude that Jewish openness as a whole is merely a response to the shift in Christianity toward the biblical pole. For, in some instances, it seems to be an opening from within. Some quarters in present-day Judaism seem to manifest the same active, initiating attitude toward dialogue that we find in biblically grounded Christianity. How is one to understand this, since our analysis has shown that the inherent position of Judaism in relation to Christianity is one of silence?

For an answer we must turn to the cultural-social conditions which characterize Jewish life in the modern world. Jewish openness can be seen as an outcome of the emancipation of Jewry into Western civilization. Emancipation signals the end of isolation. The Jew emerging from the ghetto into the mainstream of Western civilization in all its varied dimensions—economic, political, intellectual, and artistic—becomes now a child of Western culture. Since, however, Christianity is an organic dimension of Western culture the emancipated Jew confronts Christianity not only at very close quarters but, so to speak, from within. This condition of the emancipated Jew vis-à-vis Christianity has particularly far reaching consequences for Jews who happen also to be religiously concerned. For these Jews are not only in position to confront Christianity at close quarters but can also, because of their religious concern, confront it authentically as an end in itself, i.e., as a profound, alternative religious answer.

Such confrontation may lead (and indeed does lead) in two opposite directions. On the one hand, it may lead to conversion. The religiously concerned emancipated Jew may find in Christianity the answer to his yearnings and needs. His conversion is an authentic conversion of embrace. But clearly this cannot lead to the Jewish openness toward a dialogue. Since the converted Jew can no longer be a spokesman for Judaism in the dialogue with Christianity his conversion marks the end of any possibility for dialogue, not its openness. On the other hand, the confrontation with Christianity may direct the religiously concerned emancipated Jew to his own heritage. Being a product of Western culture and ignorant of his own heritage, the religiously searching Jew confronts the Christian answer. But this time instead of accepting it, the confrontation may raise in him the quest for the Jewish answer. It thus may lead him to a new anchorage in Judaism.

Such Jews, turning toward new commitment to Judaism, do not cease, however, to be the product of the Christian Western culture. They stand with one foot in the Christian Western culture and with the other in Judaism. This means openness to dialogue with that world. For openness to dialogue means awareness of, concern for and, indeed, participation in the other party. Dialogue is no longer a dispensable luxury to these emancipated Jews but a necessity, since they must come to terms with Christianity in order to secure their Jewish commitment. It is here, in this group of Jews, that the active, initiating openness to a dialogue can be detected. For these are the Jews who do seek dialogue with Christianity. The other categories of Jews do not seek the dialogue. They have no need for it, either because they have rejected the Jewish commitment of faith (the secularists), or because they live totally and exclusively within that commitment (the orthodox-ghettoized). These two categories of Jews, however, live in illusion, either the illusion of a secularized world which can include the Jews in diaspora as equals, or blindness to the reality of emancipation in Jewry which brings to Judaism the challenge of the world. Dialogically open

Jews, on the other hand, live much more authentically in the reality of our time. Although a relatively small number today, they are nevertheless very significant, for this group is coming more and more to represent Judaism in the world. To the extent that this group grows, Judaism will open itself toward actively seeking a dialogue with Christianity.

Such openness should prove to be of mutual benefit, for today, when both believing Jews and believing Christians constitute a small minority battered by a sea of nonbelievers, it is essential that they strengthen each other through the dialogue. There are differences; but there is also, and this is much more important, a common language and a common concern. According to an old rabbinic saying, God is, so to speak, nourished and strengthened when two Jews discuss matter pertaining to the Torah. Today, one should firmly believe that this is also the case when Jew and Christian discuss matters pertaining to their respective beliefs.

Although the dialogical relation of Christianity and Judaism is in many aspects predetermined by the inherent structure of the religions involved, significant room is nevertheless left in the hands of the changing historical circumstances. It is in this latter domain that human concern and decision are free to exert their influence.